THE REPAIR OF
HISTORIC BUILDINGS:
advice on
principles and methods

Christopher Brereton

1995

Copyright 1991, 1995 English Heritage

First published 1991 by English Heritage

23 Savile Row, London W1X 1AB

second edition 1995

British Library CIP data

Brereton, Christopher

The repair of historic buildings: advice on principles and methods

1. Buildings of historical importance, maintenance and repair

1. Title

690.24

ISBN 1 85074 527 7

Edited by Kate Macdonald

Designed by Typografica

Foreword to the second edition

Four years have now elapsed since *The repair of historic buildings* was prepared by the late Christopher Brereton. The volume remains a clear statement of the principles of repair generally accepted within English Heritage and only relatively minor modifications and additions to the text have been made in this second edition, together with some updating of the bibliography. As we said in 1991, each case of a historic building repair needs to be looked at on its merits, following careful analysis of the circumstances of that particular building, while the attitudes and sensitivity of building owners and their professional advisers remain as important as ever.

Philip Whitbourn
Chief Architect
English Heritage 1995

Contents

1 Introduction

The purpose of this volume is to provide guidance to building owners and their professional advisers on the principles which should be applied in the repair of historic buildings and monuments and on the methods which are appropriate to the observance of those principles.

The book has been prepared in order to satisfy a long-standing demand for such guidance from English Heritage and with the aim of achieving a consistency of approach in historic building repair.

The basic principles and objectives which are relevant to an individual case should be established at the outset and should then be applied to generate solutions to particular problems and specific methods for repair.

It is essential to identify causes before specifying remedies and in pursuit of this there is a need for a careful and accurate diagnosis including, where appropriate, monitoring of the structure.

The recommendations on methods of repair are intended for guidance only and should be considered in the context of a careful analysis of the needs of a particular building. There can be no standard specification for the repair of historic buildings and monuments.

It is important to continue to look at a building as work proceeds in case the nature of some of the repairs is found to change with the result that methods may need to be revised.

Perhaps most important of all are the attitudes and degree of sensitivity of building owners and their professional advisers, be they architects, building surveyors, structural engineers or conservators, and of those working on site.

Figs 1 (above) *and 2* (below) *Castle Bromwich Hall gardens, orangery, c1730: careful retention of all sound original fabric and accurate reinstatement of lost features in accordance with photographic evidence*

2 Principles of repair

The purpose of repair

The primary purpose of repair is to restrain the process of decay without damaging the character of buildings and monuments, altering the features which give them their historic or architectural importance, or unnecessarily disturbing or destroying historic fabric.

The need for repair

Works of repair should be kept to the minimum required to stabilise and conserve buildings and monuments, with the aim of achieving a sufficiently sound structural condition to ensure their long-term survival, and to meet the requirements of any appropriate use.

Avoiding unnecessary damage

The authenticity of an historic building or monument depends crucially on the integrity of its fabric and on its design, which may be original or may incorporate different periods of addition and alteration. The unnecessary replacement of historic fabric, no matter how carefully the work is carried out, will have an adverse effect on the appearance of a building or monument, will seriously diminish its authenticity, and will significantly reduce its value as a source of historical information. Inevitably elements of fabric will decay, or become defective in other ways, but the rate and extent to which this occurs will vary. For example, certain types of roof covering and protective wall covering will require periodic complete or major replacement. Other elements, in particular masonry and the framing of walls and roofs, are more likely to decay slowly and in parts, rather than comprehensively, and will require a more selective approach.

Fig 3 Very selective replacement and repair of timbers has preserved a large part of the original fabric of this late sixteenth-century building

Fig 4   Oxford, Botanic Gardens, gateway, 1632: replacement is restricted to the decaying weathering stones of the cornices, thus helping to slow down the rate of decay of the stonework below

Analysing historic development

A thorough understanding of the historical development of a building or monument is a necessary preliminary to its repair. This may involve archaeological and architectural investigation, documentary research, recording and interpretation of the particular structure, and its assessment in a wider historic context. Such processes may, when appropriate, need to continue during the course of repairs. It may be necessary to ask specialists in particular building types to carry out recording and analysis; measured surveys can often help other professionals in specifying repairs. Satisfactory arrangements should be made for the subsequent preservation of all records, including those of repairs carried out and of any alterations made.

Fig 5   Botching of decayed ashlar stonework with cement mortar

Analysing the causes of defects

In addition to an analysis of the historic development of the building or monument, the detailed design of repairs should also be preceded by a survey of its structural defects over as long a period as possible, together with an investigation of the nature and condition of its materials and of the causes,

Fig 6 A policy of replacement rather than repair has resulted in loss of historic integrity, despite accurate copying of details

appearance and historic integrity of the building or monument, and to ensure tha repairs have an appropriate life. Exceptions should only be considered where the existing fabric has failed because of inherent defects of design or incorrect specification of materials, rather than from neglect of maintenance or because it has completed its expected life. New methods and techniques should only be used where they have proved themselves over a sufficient period, and where traditional alternatives cannot be identified, or where the use of modern methods enables important features to be retained. In deciding whether to adopt new methods and techniques it will be necessary to balance the degree of benefit to the building or monument in the future against any damage which may be caused to its appearance or historic integrity and fabric.

processes, and rates of decay. To repair or replace decayed fabric without first carrying out such an investigation is to invite the repetition of problems.

Adopting proven techniques

In making repairs, the aim should be to match existing materials and methods of construction, in order to preserve the

Fig 7 Adopting the correct priority for repairs: the stone-slated roof has been relaid using existing materials and replacing defective slates to match; the wall framing is thus protected and its repair may follow in due course

Truth to materials

Repairs should be executed honestly, usually without attempt at disguise or artificial ageing, but should not be unnecessarily obtrusive or unsympathetic in appearance. When the replacement of historic fabric is unavoidably extensive, or significant in other ways, the work may be discreetly dated for future reference.

Removal of later alterations

Additions or alterations, including earlier repairs, can be of importance for the part they play in the cumulative history of a building or monument. There should therefore be a strong presumption in favour of their retention. While a programme of repairs may offer the opportunity for removing features which are of no intrinsic value in themselves, and which seriously disrupt the architectural design and aesthetic value of a building or monument, the full implications of doing so must be carefully considered in advance, and potential architectural and aesthetic gains need to be balanced against any likely loss of historic integrity. Work of this kind should be carefully measured and recorded and the necessary statutory consents must be obtained in advance.

Restoration of lost features

Some elements of a building or monument which are important to its design, for example balustrades, pinnacles, cornices, hoodmoulds, window tracery, and members of a timber frame or roof truss, may have been lost in the past. Where these are of structural significance, they will normally be replacedbe in the course of repair; but a

Figs 8 (below left) *and 9* (right) *The East Banqueting House, Chipping Camden: the replacement, as part of a comprehensive programme of repair, of a missing corner chimneystack which was an important part of the original design of the building*

programme of repair may also offer the opportunity for the reinstatement of missing non-structural elements, provided that sufficient evidence exists for accurate replacement, no loss of historic fabric occurs, and the necessary statutory consents are obtained in advance. Speculative reconstruction is hardly ever justified.

Safeguarding the future

An historic building or monument should be regularly monitored and maintained, and, wherever possible, provided with an appropriate and sympathetic use. This is the best way of securing its future, and of keeping further repair requirements to a minimum.

Fig 10   Ettington Park, Warwickshire, 1858–62, architect John Prichard. This house was once in a state of near dereliction. Stonework was carefully selected to match the polycromy of the original work, with minimum replacement

3 Maintenance and minor repairs

The best means of ensuring the continued preservation of a building is to carry out regular maintenance. Such work is part of the day-to-day responsibility of all owners and occupiers.

Maintenance most crucially concerns those elements which protect a building from water and damp penetration, in particular roof coverings, gutters, downpipes, gullies and perimeter drains, and also open joints in masonry, cracked render, etc.

The best means of monitoring the need for and effectiveness of maintenance, and also of assessing when major repairs are required, is to institute a system of periodic detailed inspection of the building by a suitably qualified professional who will prepare a report with recommendations. Such an inspection should be carried out at least every five years. The preparation and regular updating of a maintenance and repair diary, supplemented with key drawings, photographs, etc will be a valuable source of reference for all those responsible for a building now and in the future.

Maintenance may be divided into two main categories; first, that which depends on the day-to-day vigilance of the building owner and can usually be dealt with without the need to employ outside labour; and second, that which is in the nature of minor repair and is best carried out on an annual basis by a builder who has knowledge of and sympathy towards historic building construction. It should be noted, however, that even such relatively minor works will benefit from being overseen by a qualified professional. Expenditure on fees is usually offset by improved cost control and a higher standard of work, with longer-lasting effects.

Day-to-day maintenance

Clearing leaves
Clear leaves, accumulated silt, etc from gutters (including parapet and valley gutters), flat roofs, downpipes, gullies, perimeter drainage channels, etc. This should be done about once every three months and particularly during and after the autumn fall of leaves. This is probably the single most important operation and if neglected will soon be the cause of major defects. Faults in rainwater goods, etc are most readily identified during heavy rain. Where access is difficult, fixed ladders, hatches, etc should be installed in convenient but unobtrusive positions.

Clearing snow
Clearing snow from valley and parapet gutters, flat roofs, etc to prevent it from building up above the level of sheet laps and flashings and to prevent water which is thawing below snow from refreezing and blocking outlets. Wooden or plastic shovels should be used, but great care is needed to avoid damaging leadwork, slating, etc (it should be noted that electric heating tapes can be an effective means of helping to keep flat roofs and valley and parapet gutters clear).

Fig 11 Accumulation of silt and leaves in this lead valley gutter and plant growth on the roof tiling indicates serious lack of attention to day-to-day maintenance

Controlling plant growth

Plant growth on masonry and around the perimeter of the building should be controlled and removed where this is injurious. This should be done at an early stage before roots get a hold and penetrate deeply into a wall. If ivy has been allowed to grow, it should be killed by cutting through the stem near the ground and applying a poisonous paste. The upper part should be left to die before it is carefully detached from the wall. Alternatively, poisoning the ivy through its root system may more effectively ensure that the root is killed.

Fig 12 Ivy has caused extensive damage to the face of this flint wall

When plant growth is removed from the ground around the perimeter of a building, it is important to ensure that the ground level is maintained so as not to allow either the progressive exposure of the wall base and foundations, or the build-up of ground levels.

Removing bird droppings

Remove accumulations of bird droppings. Internally, in the church towers, attics, etc droppings can cause timber decay. Loose bird guards should be refixed to prevent access. (Arrangements should be made for defective guards to be replaced in non-ferrous or plastic material). Externally, on masonry, droppings can produce damaging salts. Care should be taken to observe the necessary health and safety precautions when removing bird droppings.

Looking for insect and fungal attack

Check for signs of active insect or fungal attack in timbers and, if this is suspected, inform your architect or an independent consultant. A specialist firm, which has a vested interest in carrying out treatment, may recommend more extensive treatment than is strictly necessary (see *Repair of structural timbers*).

Checking ventilation

Ensure that ventilators are kept open within the body of a building and in roof voids, although in the latter case the need to compartmentalise roof voids and attics in large buildings to prevent the spread of fire should be taken into account. Good ventilation is particularly important to help prevent condensation and outbreaks of fungal attack, both of which are encouraged by modern demands for increased thermal comfort. (If ventilation is inadequate, arrangements should be made for it to be provided by simple and unobtrusive means, eg by incorporating bronze mesh within the glazing pattern of a window, or by forming slots at the eaves, or, if natural means are not feasible, by installing small humidistat-controlled ventilator units.)

Minor repairs and maintenance involving builder's works

Minor works to slate and tile roofs

Patch repairs should be carried out by refixing loose and slipped slates and tiles and replacing broken ones with matching material.

Excess moss should be carefully removed as this can harbour damp, causing slates and tiles to laminate (see also *Repair of existing leadwork and other metal coverings*).

Bitumen-coated fabric applied over roofs or spray-on coating systems on the underside of roofs should not be used. They prevent sound slates or tiles from being salvaged for reuse when comprehensive roof repairs are eventually undertaken. Also, when subsequent defects occur, they are difficult to locate and make good. Such treatments may also have the effect of sealing roof voids and preventing ventilation, with the consequent risk of fungal attack and rot of roof timbers.

Repair of existing leadwork and other metal coverings

Individual worn-out sheets should be replaced and splits in roofs and gutters which have some years of life remaining should be repaired before complete stripping and renewal become necessary. Apart from emergency temporary patches with strips of adhesive tape, holes and splits should be properly repaired with lead-welded patches, not by the use of solder. This should be carried out by a qualified plumber and stringent fire precautions should be observed. Bitumen-coated fabrics or other bitumenised treatments should not be used. They conceal later developing faults in the lead and inhibit the carrying out of permanent repairs. Their effective life is short as exposure to ultra-violet radiation results in degradation. In addition, they substantially reduce the credit value of the old lead because of the cost of removing the coatings which is a difficult and labour-intensive process.

Fig 13 Maintenance of this slate roof has been botched which will cause difficulties for those wishing to carry out the work to a correct standard in the future

Fig 14 'Rippling' of oversized bays of lead caused by expansion and contraction which will lead to fatigue cracking, an example of which has been unsuitably repaired with solder

Rain falling on moss or lichen-covered slate or tile roofs discharges as an acidic run-off, causing holes or channels in metal roof coverings below. Sacrificial flashings may be provided where the run-off occurs, or, as an additional precaution, copper wire may be fixed across the roof slope in order to create a copper salt wash during rainfall which will inhibit the growth of moss or lichen.

Copper, stainless steel, or aluminium roofs are, because of their lighter weight, more prone to damage by wind-lift. Should such damage occur, it should be dealt with immediately by refixing at seams or ridges, otherwise cracking and general failure, caused by 'working' in the wind, may necessitate complete replacement. Other minor defects may be temporarily dealt with by fixing patches of matching metal secured by a waterproof adhesive.

Refixing slipped lead or other metal flashings

This will be necessary at gable and chimney abutments, parapets, etc, as will be the replacement of short lengths of flashing in matching material where they are split or holed. Vertical splits may be covered with matching material and wedged and pointed above the original flashing (see *Metal roof coverings*).

Maintenance of thatch

Thatch may be long straw, combed wheat reed, or water reed. Roofs should be regularly inspected and local repairs, including any necessary re-ridging, carried out in a matching material by an experienced thatcher (see *Thatch*).

Maintenance of eaves gutters and downpipes

Maintenance includes the de-rusting and painting of cast-iron rainwater goods and replacement of short, broken, and split lengths in matching material, not in pvc. Rectangular cast-iron downpipes should be particularly carefully maintained as they are liable to rust unseen at the back. Downpipes should be repainted and refixed on spacers sufficiently clear of the wall to allow for a free flow of air and also for inspection and painting.

Where downpipes are connected directly into drains (ie without gullies) they are liable to become blocked, allowing the pipes to fill with water and freeze, causing cracking. Gullies should therefore be provided (*not* back-inlet) in order to allow for the rodding of rainwater pipes and drains.

Fig 16   The coating of this defective lead parapet gutter with bitumen will make the identification of further faults difficult and also reduce the credit value of the lead when it is eventually replaced

Fig 15   Careful maintenance of an old lead roof: shown by a lead-welded patch to a split roll end

Cast-iron gutters which sit on stone-corbelled eaves courses are particularly vulnerable to rusting on their undersides and backs and it may be wise to wedge them up clear of the stone to allow evaporation of moisture below. Where joints have failed, the gutter should be dismantled to remake them and, before reinstating, a flashing may be laid under the gutter as an additional precaution.

Lead downpipes, hopper heads, and sometimes cast-iron hopper heads can be of historic interest or important features of a building and, if damaged, should be carefully overhauled rather than replaced (see *Renewal of rainwater goods*).

Faults in rainwater goods will soon lead to saturation of adjacent areas of wall. Overflows are useful to direct spillage away from the building and in indicating where there are blocked heads and pipes. If maintenance is neglected mortar will be washed out of joints in masonry, plant growth will develop, and serious structural problems may arise. Moisture transference to the interior can cause significant damage and is usually the cause of dry or wet rot originating in associated timber.

Maintenance of perimeter drainage channels or ground gutters

These are most commonly found around churches and are often a source of trouble, since cracks or open joints will allow considerable amounts of water to seep into the foundations (affecting their stability in due course), and will also cause rising damp in walls (affecting internal finishes and fittings). Cracks should, therefore, be pointed wherever they occur, but it is preferable to remove channels and replace them with a system of gullies below the downpipes, connected to drains.

Rodding and subsequent inspection of underground stormwater drains

Any necessary minor repairs should be made to short lengths of drain.

Fig 17 Unless this rusting rectangular cast-iron downpipe and blocked hopper head are dealt with, the adjacent brickwork will be seriously damaged by water saturation and put at risk any timbers built into the structure

Minor areas of repointing of stonework and brickwork

Small, isolated areas of repointing should be dealt with regularly as items of maintenance, but only where joints are open or mortar is loose; *sound old pointing should always be left undisturbed.* It is important that repointing is correctly carried out using a lime mortar, *not* a cement mortar, to avoid damage to the appearance and character, as well as the structure of a building. Inappropriate mortar mixes and finishes of joint in pointing can cause major disfigurement to the appearance of a building.

Maintenance of external render

Old lime renders and daubs, sometimes self-finished in the case of the former, and often limewashed in the case of the latter, have an attractive character and may be of historical interest. Their life should be prolonged for as long as possible by correct maintenance, with patch repairs in a carefully matched mix to cracked or loose areas, and, when appropriate, by regular re-limewashing.

Harder renders used in the nineteenth and twentieth centuries also need regular maintenance if they are not to fail rapidly due to water penetration through cracks. They are often painted, but where they are self-finished a successful match of colour and texture may be difficult, and is best achieved by the correct choice of sand.

Additions of pigment may, however, sometimes be necessary, although these tend to fade and weather differently in time (see *Repair of external render* for advice on repair of renders).

Preventative treatment of timber against insect and fungal attack

Prevention is best achieved by ensuring that the timber is kept dry and well ventilated.

When insect attack occurs, it can be kept at bay by the periodic use of insecticides at the time of emergence of the insect in the spring; in addition preventative action may be taken by the avoidance of warm, poorly ventilated spaces which encourage breeding. If preservative fluids are used these should be colourless and care taken to avoid damage to historic surfaces and decorative treatments. Also, they should be non-toxic to bats when these are present in a building, and English Nature must be consulted prior to embarking in treatment (see *Repair of structural timbers*).

Minor repairs to small areas of internal plaster and associated redecoration

New plaster should be carefully matched in mix and finish to the old (see *Repair of plain and decorative plasterwork* for advice on repair of plaster). Internal decoration of plaster finishes to solid walls should never be undertaken using plastic paint as this will form an impervious skin and is foreign to an ancient building.

Minor glazing repairs

These include replacement of individual broken panes (or, where feasible and appropriate, their retention by fitting additional cames), support of deformed leaded panels, removal of organic growth, etc. Where glass is of historic importance, even minor works should be entrusted to a specialist conservator of glass (see *Repair of glass* for advice on repair of glazing).

Regular painting of external woodwork

Associated fittings, such as door and window hinges, should also be properly maintained.

Fig 18 Unless dealt with, the left-hand cornice and wall surface will rapidly deteriorate and require extensive repair

4 Methods of repair

Works to secure general structural stability

Preliminary investigation

Leaning walls, cracks in masonry, etc may be symptoms of foundation settlement or other structural movement of long standing which may have now stabilised. Before any action is taken, therefore, it is necessary to understand the building structure and monitor the situation over a period of time in order to determine whether or not it is of sufficient seriousness to warrant action being taken. Monitoring should, wherever possible, be in excess of one year in order to take account of ordinary seasonal variations in movement.

Specialist structural engineering advice is required on the need for monitoring and for any subsequent repairs. An engineer experienced in dealing with historic buildings should be chosen. It should also be noted in the context of work of this nature that Codes of Practice, building regulations, and contemporary standards are not necessarily applicable.

Where repairs are required, either in order to deal with defects caused by past movement which has now ceased, or where movement is still active, the aim should be, wherever possible, to stabilise and strengthen *in situ*, unless distortion or

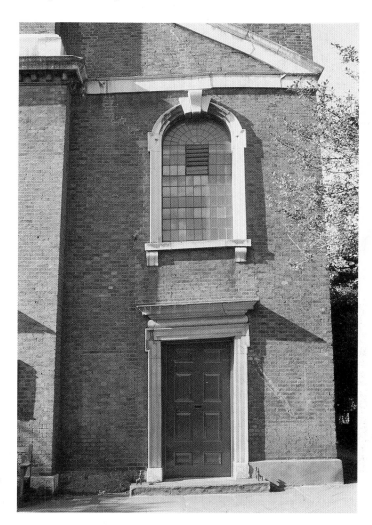

Fig 19   Distortion of a building by settlement may be of long standing and monitoring may be needed before it can be decided whether structural repairs are required

weakening of the structure is so far advanced that partial dismantling and rebuilding are unavoidable. In the latter case, the work should be preceded by a full drawn and photographic record in order to ensure an accurate rebuilding. Components of the building should be numbered to correspond with numbers on drawings.

Stabilisation of foundations

Shallow foundations on shrinkable clays can be affected by cyclical expansion and contraction of the clay around the periphery of a building, causing differential settlement. This may be affected by the presence of trees, particularly in areas of friable clay. It may be possible to stabilise the water level in the soil by providing a French drain falling to soakaways or to a nearby watercourse, if available; however, changes in ground conditions brought about by the introduction of drainage may themselves have undesirable effects, so engineering advice should always be obtained. If movement has already seriously affected the structure, however, it may be necessary to consider more radical measures such as underpinning the foundation below the level at which saturation takes place. Partial or intermittent underpinning should be avoided, as this is likely to settle differentially.

Another possible cause of foundation failure is ground settlement due to the compression of soft fill in ditches, pits, etc from previous human activity on a site.

Subsidence due to new mining is less likely to occur than in the past and adequate notice should have been given so that appropriate measures, such as the installation of a reinforced concrete raft, may be taken in advance and at the expense of the mining operator.

Because of the risks posed to the archaeological record within the ground, such works will often require supervision by an archaeologist. Advice on this should be obtained from English Heritage.

Repair of leaning walls

Foundations affected by differential settlement of the ground at the periphery of a building may cause walls to lean outwards, possibly with associated cracking at the corners of openings, pulling of floor beams and roof trusses from their bearing, etc. Each case will require careful analysis before a decision is made on a method of repair.

In exceptional circumstances, where serious failure has occurred, one possible method of repair may be the introduction of a reinforced concrete wall-top beam returned at either end and linked to vertical

Fig 20   Opening up during repair work exposed serious structural cracking in this cross wall. Subsequent investigation showed that this was due to foundation failure

Fig 21   The crack above the lower window may be the result of a failed lintel but careful opening up at the rear will be necessary to determine whether this is the case or whether other structural weaknesses are playing their part

reinforced posts, contained within the thickness of the wall. The posts would then be attached to horizontal members running back inside the building below floor level. Care should, however, be taken over proposals for introducing such rigid elements into relatively flexible structures and the extent of their use in a particular case should be kept to the minimum required. In some circumstances a less · drastic (and potentially reversible) type of repair may be made using steel sections, provided this can be achieved relatively unobtrusively. Alternatively, the insertion of tie-bars to fix one wall to its neighbour, and to connect walls to the diaphragm action of floors and to any strong points at roof level, may suffice in some circumstances.

The addition of conventional buttresses is normally to be avoided as these can settle independently, either falling away from the wall or pulling it over further.

A masonry wall may be leaning because of foundation failure to an extent which threatens collapse. It may sometimes be possible to bring it back towards the vertical by forming a horizontal chase on the inside near the base, in order to form a 'hinge'. The foundation would then be reformed as necessary and a framework and/or shoring erected on the outside face of the wall. The wall would then be pulled back from behind by anchored steel cables, followed by the reinstatement of the chase.

In cases where walls lean for reasons other than foundation failure, eg roof thrust, they may be anchored to floor beams or tie beams (following any necessary repairs to the roof structure) using straps and plates. Another method may be to install tie rods across the width of the building or to major internal walls.

Cracks and unstable cores

Cracks in walls caused by movement need to be dealt with in accordance with the degree of structural seriousness. It is necessary to determine whether failure is due to compression or tension, since treatment may involve a different approach or technique.

Minor cracks may only require pointing. More serious ones may be repaired by stitching across the crack using material matching the wall construction, or by setting reinforced concrete stitches behind the face. Another method may be to insert non-ferrous metal ties in bed joints. Diagonal pinning across a crack with threaded stainless steel rods set in a resin grout may be an appropriate method in some circumstances.

Pinning may also be used in conjunction with the grouting of rubble core filling where

Fig 22 Thin facing stones forced away from a loose rubble core. It will be necessary to build up the collapsed parts of the core and the face, then consolidate the core with grout and pin the facing stones into it

this has become loose, and also where the face has bulged away from the core. The mix for the grout and method of application will vary according to the particular circumstances (eg hand poured, gravity pumped, or by vacuum). The decision on whether or not to carry out grouting should be carefully considered in terms of the effect it will have on the loading and flexibility of a wall.

It is particularly important that works involving the introduction of new components within the structure of a building are properly recorded and the information made accessible for future reference.

Recovering of roofs

When a roof is stripped for recovering it is important that any necessary repairs to the roof structure are carried out at the same time (see *Repair of structural timbers*), together with other associated work at roof level, such as gutters, chimneystacks, parapets, gables, dormers, rooflights, etc. This averts the need for the later disturbance of recently laid roof finishes and makes the most economical use of scaffolding.

Unless there is a good reason not to, roof coverings should be replaced on a like-for-like basis. Possible exceptions are discussed under the separate sections below.

Slates, stone slates, and clay tiles including pantiles

Failure is usually caused by the corrosion of nails fixing slates or tiles to battens, the decay of battens, and the lamination of cracking of slates or tiles.

When recovering, it is advisable to photograph the roof prior to stripping, to ensure that the existing details are properly followed.

Stripping should be carried out carefully to ensure that all sound existing slates or tiles remain undamaged so that they may be sorted according to type, size, and thickness and stored ready for reuse. When assessing existing slates or tiles for reuse, their likely further life should be carefully considered.

Unevenness of a roof surface is often part of the character of an old roof and unless it is likely to affect weather tightness, no attempt should be made to level up for the sake of creating an even surface.

Except in exposed conditions, where driving snow is likely to penetrate under slates or tiles, it is generally preferable not to use sarking felt because this is likely to inhibit the free flow of air which is possible without it. If its use can be sufficiently justified, a breather felt should be used and other means of ventilating the roof timbers should be introduced (eg at the eaves) in order to reduce the risk of decay and fungal attack. Sarking felt should not be used, however, in cases where it is appropriate that the underside of the slates or tiles are visible within a building, eg barns and some other types of vernacular or early industrial buildings. Where mortar torching exists in such cases it should normally be kept and repaired or replaced as necessary, but in other cases it is not recommended in re-roofing.

Fig 23 Ventilation of a roof void has been unobtrusively incorporated in this lead ridge-capping to a slated roof

Replacement battens or laths should be pre-treated against fungal attack. They should preferably be fixed to rafters with ringed stainless steel nails, as galvanised steel has a shorter life. Riven oak or chestnut laths should be used where they already exist, or, if not, where they are nevertheless appropriate to the date and type of building, and particularly where the underside of a roof is visible within a building.

Reslating or retiling should be carried out using sound slates or tiles salvaged from the roof, with any deficiencies made up with new or sound secondhand materials, matching the existing ones in type, size, thickness, colour, and texture. The selection of existing slates or tiles for reuse should be carried out with great care to ensure that they will have a significant life in relation to new material.

Substitute materials such as artificial slates made of fibre resin, artificial stone slates made of 'reconstituted stone',

Fig 24 These replacement tiles have not been matched in colour and texture to the existing ones

concrete tiles, etc are not appropriate. Handmade clay tiles should not be replaced with machine-made ones, nor pantiles with plain tiles. Conversely, machine-made tiles should not be replaced with handmade ones where they form part of the original character of the building.

If the existing slates or tiles are themselves an inappropriate earlier replacement, it may be appropriate to reinstate the original material provided that accurate evidence of

Fig 25 However cleverly made they may be, artificial stone slates are recognisable for what they are

its previous use exists and that a significant proportion of the later material is in sufficiently poor condition to need replacing.

The use of material cannibalised from other old buildings should be avoided wherever possible. New stone slates and handmade tiles can usually be obtained and this has the advantage of encouraging production of these materials.

It is preferable in some cases that sound old slates or tiles are laid together on visible slopes, with new ones kept for less prominent slopes and inner slopes of valleys, etc. In other cases it is important to maintain the existing colour and texture of the roofs by mixing tiles judiciously.

When using new stone slates, hand dressing will often be necessary to ensure good bedding and to remove the mechanical appearance of machine-finished sides and tails.

Slates and stone slates, with the exception of Welsh slates since the late eighteenth century and often Delaboles, have almost always been laid in courses diminishing in size from the eaves to the ridge and this should be carefully matched in recovering. When stripping, care should be taken to sort and stack the courses.

Fixing nails for slates and tiles should preferably be stout copper. Stainless steel nails are a possible alternative but it should be noted that they may be difficult to remove when repairs are necessary. Only nails with large-diameter shanks should be considered, otherwise they will tend to cut through the slate in time. Galvanised, plated, or plain steel nails should not be used. Where wooden pegs or cast-iron pins have been used for slates, stone slates, or tiles on internally exposed roofs of barns, etc, they should be replaced to match. Wooden pegs should be treated, following shaping, against pest and fungal attack.

Details on roofs, such as ridge and hip coverings, eaves, verges, valleys, etc will vary according to the roof covering, the building type and its period, regional variations, etc. They should be replaced in their existing form, except where inappropriate and unsympathetic earlier changes have been made, in which case they should preferably be reinstated in their original form, provided there is sufficient evidence for this.

Some components are particularly valuable, eg ornamental ridge or hip coverings of clay, lead, or iron, often with finials at the ends, or stone and slate ridges

Fig 26   Good practice in recovering a roof of sandstone flags, correctly laid in diminishing courses (photo Leeds City Council)

of various kinds. Existing sections are very often capable of reuse, but if beyond repair they should be carefully remade in a matching material and design.

Lead soakers and flashings should be provided at abutments of roofs with gables, chimneystacks, etc, although in some cases other, locally traditional details should be retained where they exist, eg a mortar fillet in a soft lime mix (but provided with lead soakers below) protected by a projecting course of brick or stone, or by tile creasing. The chasing of old masonry for new flashings should be avoided where possible.

Vertical slate hanging on walls, particularly on late Georgian buildings, is often found in the south west and parts of the north west, and in many seaside towns, as a protection against wind-driven, salt-laden rain. Clay tile hanging and mathematical tiles to simulate brickwork on late eighteenth- and nineteenth-century timber-framed structures are quite often found in the south-eastern counties. Details and decorative treatments and methods of fixing will vary according to material and locality and should usually, where possible, be carefully matched in repairs. Replacement battens should be pre-treated, fixing nails should be non-ferrous or of stainless steel, and concealed lead soakers should be introduced to protect junctions at corners and between vertical surfaces and roof slopes, etc.

Metal roof coverings

Lead

Where very old lead survives on roofs, particularly any medieval lead which may occasionally be found on small roofs such as church porches and towers, it should be regarded as a valuable part of the fabric of the building and wherever possible should be kept and repaired rather than replaced. Such work may involve refixing slipped sheets, possibly replacing some which are worn out, reforming details of rolls, flashings, etc, and repairing splits and holes with lead-welded patches, including the

Fig 27   Leadwork of great age which should, if practicably possible, be retained and carefully repaired by lead-welded patches (not solder as shown)

replacement by lead welding of ineffective soldered repairs. Strict fire precautions should be observed during the carrying out of such work.

Repair rather than complete replacement may also be appropriate for later lead roofs. If, however, inherent faults exist in a lead roof or gutter linings, such as oversized or overfixed sheets leading to damage caused by thermal movement, insufficient fixing causing slipping, poorly detailed drips or rolls, etc, which have been a constant source of trouble necessitating regular repair, then complete replacement will be required. Names and dates cast into the sheets of an old roof or old graffiti may be of interest and worth saving and welding on to the new one.

New leadwork should be specified correctly in respect of sizes of sheet and thickness, falls, and details of joints and

Fig 28   An old lead roof which is clearly well past its life, showing over-long sheets which have slipped and several solder repairs

Fig 29   Good modern practice in leadwork

fixings. The thickness of lead for pitched roofs, flat roofs, and gutter linings should not be less than Code 7; for vertical cladding, Code 6; for flashings and hip and ridge cappings, Code 5; and for soakers, Code 4. Compliance with current standards for sheet sizes will often entail reforming the substrate. Sand-cast lead is normally to be preferred when replacing historic material.

Occasionally, it may be proposed that a timber gutter base be replaced with concrete. This should normally be avoided, however, and should only be considered as a possibility where the timber is in need of major renewal due to rot, or where major reconstruction of the gutter is needed in order to provide correct falls, sheet sizes, etc. Otherwise, the existing construction should be kept and repaired as necessary. If concrete is decided upon, it must also be possible to isolate fully any structural timbers from the concrete by an air gap of at least 25mm on three sides to prevent the development of rot. Merely wrapping timbers in polythene, etc is not sufficient. Expansion joints should be provided in the concrete on the line of each drip.

Corrosion caused by condensation on the underside of lead on roofs has become a problem of increasing concern. It is often found where the internal environment of a building has been changed by the installation of central heating or intermittent systems of heating and where there is inadequate general ventilation. This situation is worsened when associated with leadwork of non-traditional design which does not allow ventilation to the underside of the lead, thereby preventing condensation from evaporating and thus accelerating corrosion.

In some cases a roof which was originally lead clad may have been recovered at a later date with another material, usually for cheapness, eg Welsh slates. Sometimes the roof pitch is too low for the substitute material to function adequately and, when the time arrives for its replacement, on both technical and historical grounds it may be appropriate to revert to lead.

Stainless steel

In cases where there has been a persistent history of the theft of lead from a roof and it can be shown that all reasonable security measures have been tried and have failed, then use of an alternative material may be considered, subject to approval. It should be noted, however, that where lead is a prominent feature of the design and appearance of a building, it is unlikely that any other material would be appropriate.

Where it is agreed that an alternative material to lead may be used, dull-finished stainless steel can be a possible substitute provided that the roof is hidden by parapets, etc. Although the detailing of stainless steel is different from lead, similar sheet widths should be chosen for the sake of appearance. Due to the difficult workability of stainless steel it may be necessary to use lead for some complicated junctions, flashing, etc and possibly also to retain lead for gutters.

Where a roof is visible from below, terne-coated stainless steel should be used.

Copper

In the past, copper was sometimes introduced as a replacement for lead, and, although the problem of pitch does not arise, it is usually preferable, when the copper has reached the end of its life, to reinstate lead on the grounds that it is historically and visually appropriate, subject to the roof being capable of bearing its weight and the conditions right.

When copper was the original material, however, it is often important to the design intention, and when replacement is necessary it should be on a like-for-like basis.

Detailed specifications for copper roofing should ensure that bay sizes, weight, and fixing details are correct so as to minimise the risk of damage by wind lift, thermal movement, and condensation.

Thatch

When rethatching, it is important to maintain regional characteristics of material and of general form and detail. The materials most commonly in use today are long straw, combed wheat reed, water reed, and sedge for ridges. There may sometimes be reasons for reinstating thatch on a building that was originally thatched but was later re-roofed with another material.

As examples of regional appearance, East Anglian roofs tend to be in regular planes, with steep pitches, pointed gables with rolled verges, and often with decorative ridges, etc, while in the West Country shapes are softer in outline and lower in pitch, with half-hipped gables with rounded verges, and a general lack of ornamental features. In order to ensure that such regional features are not lost when rethatching, an experienced thatcher should be employed who works in accordance with local tradition. Old photographs, etc may be consulted in order to ensure accurate reinstatement of original features.

Complete stripping is rarely needed; only defective thatch should be removed to a sound base. Sometimes original layers may survive below, possibly retaining valuable historical evidence, such as smoke-blackened thatch and timbers in domestic roofs, surviving from the time when there was a louvre before a chimneystack was inserted, and even the remains of a louvre. Care should be taken to ensure that such features remain undisturbed.

Fig 30 Thatching in progress: note the use of underlay, which is not recommended

A woven mat visible between the rafters of some early roofs, and known as 'fleeking', should be retained during rethatching.

Felt underlay or polythene sheeting should not be used for thatched roofs as it will inhibit drying out.

If anti-fire devices are introduced for thatch, they should be visually acceptable.

Occasionally examples of heather thatch or ling may be found to survive and should be preserved and repaired to match by craftsmen familiar with the material and techniques used.

Shingles

Shingles are traditionally of cleft oak. If the materials are properly selected and fixed a shingle roof should have a life of up to 70 years. Sawn cedar shingles are a less appropriate alternative, being larger and dull and flat in appearance. Cleft sweet chestnut shingles may be another alternative, being of the correct size, and after weathering, a reasonable match in appearance and texture. As they are made from young trees, however, both edges are likely to contain sapwood so preservative treatment by pressure impregnation is necessary. Replacement shingles should not be lighter in weight than the original ones.

As shingles need adequate ventilation underneath, felt underlay should not be used, except for particularly exposed situations, where a breather felt is advisable.

If pre-drilled to prevent splitting, shingles may be fixed by stout copper nails; alternatively, two thin stainless steel nails may be used without pre-drilling. Galvanised steel nails should not be used.

Where there is a risk of attack by woodpeckers, a strip of zinc may be inserted behind each course of shingles.

Asphalt

Recovering in asphalt is appropriate where this is the original material, eg on concrete roofs. The works should be carried out in accordance with the best current practice.

Where, however, asphalt has earlier been laid on a timber roof which was originally covered with lead, then lead should normally be reinstated when the asphalt has reached the end of its life. Timber is not a satisfactory base for asphalt.

Dormers and skylights

Dormers vary in from the simple 'cat-slide' type clad with slate or tile, to architecturally important features with pediments of stone or moulded timber, covered with lead, and with lead cheeks. All details should be carefully followed in repairs. Any lost features of significance or unsympathetic alterations should be made good *provided sufficiently accurate evidence exists*, either from adjacent dormers or from old photographs and drawings, eg the lead covering a pediment may later have been inappropriately replaced with tiles, or the glazing bars of windows may have been lost.

Skylights also vary widely in size and degree of elaboration, depending on the building type and whether or not they are intended to be significant elements of the design, either when seen externally or from an important internal space such as a staircase. When repairs are carried out, materials, usually timber or iron, and details of mouldings, glazing bars, etc, should be carefully matched. Although it may sometimes be necessary to improve weather tightness by modifying flashings, etc, this should be done unobtrusively. Old glass, including coloured or patterned glass sometimes found in nineteenth-century skylights, should always be carefully retained during repairs.

Plain, iron-framed skylights set below the plane of the roof should not be replaced with a modern type with different details. Exceptions may only possibly be considered where a skylight is completely hidden from external view on inner slopes, etc, and where it is not visible from important internal spaces. Such an alteration would require statutory consent.

Renewal of rainwater goods

Cracked or broken cast-iron gutters and downpipes should be replaced in matching material and section, eg half-round, box, or ogee gutters, and round or rectangular section downpipes, etc. In the case of some complicated sections it may be feasible and economical to repair the existing ones by welding. Substitute materials such as pvc or extruded aluminium are not appropriate, although painted cast aluminium may be considered in cases where gutters and downpipes are very high on a building or otherwise particularly difficult of access, so that sufficiently regular painting cannot be carried out. Sound existing lengths of cast iron should be reused after de-rusting. Special castings may be needed for some lengths if unobtainable from stock. If an existing system is functionally deficient in certain locations, eg undersized gutters or downpipes, unable to cope with heavy rain, then it may be necessary to fit larger components, but they should be of the same design and not so much larger as significantly to affect the appearance of the building. Some deficiencies may be overcome by the introduction of an extra downpipe, the location of which should be approved.

Downpipes should be fitted on spacers far enough from the wall that if a leak should occur water will run down the back of the pipe and not down the wall. This will also allow a free flow of air round the pipe to inhibit the development of rust and access for repainting the back. Fixings should also allow for ease of dismantling.

Where there are sensitive internal features, such as wall paintings, it may be prudent to consider resiting downpipes away from them.

Lead downpipes, rainwater heads, and gutters should, wherever possible, be overhauled by reforming sagged or dented sections and repairing splits by lead welding, not soldering. When sections are beyond repair they should be replaced in a matching weight of lead, and to the same design. Iron fixings should not be used.

In circumstances where there is persistent theft or vandalism, consideration may be given to the replacement of the lowest or most accessible sections of lead downpipes in a substitute material such as terne-coated stainless steel or, possibly, in appropriate circumstances, cast iron.

Rainwater heads should be fitted with overflows where these do not already exist and where they will not interfere with a fine design. Water chutes on high roofs should be of sufficient projection to prevent water from falling against the building.

Wooden gutters, chutes, or downpipes should be repaired in matching timber to the same design. Elm is a traditional material for gutters as it swells rapidly when wet and prevents leakage. Where appropriate, gutters may be lined with lead, if proper jointing is feasible; if not, coating internally with bitumen is a traditional method.

Fig 31   A defective lead downpipe, which was causing considerable damage to the stonework, has been replaced, but unfortunately in pvc

Fig 32   A leaking cast-iron downpipe which washed out the joints of adjacent brickwork has been properly replaced in cast iron (unfortunately the brickwork has been poorly repaired)

Fig 33 The installation of a French drain around the perimeter of a church where damp had been causing serious damage to internal plaster. Excavations for such work should always be monitored by an archaeologist

Repair or installation of surface water drainage

Downpipes should discharge over gullies (not back-inlet; see *Maintenance of eaves gutters and downpipes*), which should be connected to drains running, if possible, to a nearby watercourse or to main drains. If these are not available, properly designed soakaways should be constructed at a distance from the gilding. Catch pits and rodding eyes should be incorporated in the system.

It is not satisfactory for a downpipe to discharge into a perimeter drainage channel as the concentration of water on one spot is likely to wash away mortar from joints in the channel and cause seepage of water into foundations and rising damp in the wall.

Perimeter channels are common around churches, either at ground level or sunk into a 'dry area', and having surfaces of brick, tile, or stone. Such channels are not always very satisfactory, as they often give very little support beneath the surfaces, which are liable to settle and crack away from the wall. This, in turn, lets water in and the surfaces resist drying out. Where such a channel exists, therefore, and is in need of major repair, it is preferable to remove it and install another system, eg a French drain connected to a watercourse or soakaway. This may not be possible, however, where there are shallow foundations. It should also be noted that a French drain must be correctly installed and properly maintained, otherwise there is a risk that it may block and allow water to collect against the foundations. To prevent this from happening, the trench should be filled to the top with stones or gravel. The archaeological implications of such work should be taken into account and in the case of churches the diocesan archaeological advisor should be consulted.

Prevention of rising damp and associated problems

Walls

Only when rising damp is causing significant deterioration, particularly if salts are also present, will it usually be necessary to take measures to prevent it. Particular care should, however, be taken to ensure that damp is kept away from built-in timbers.

Before any measures are taken the problem should be analysed in order to identify the cause properly. In the first instance professional advice should be obtained, rather than that of a specialist contractor. Dampness may occur in walls because of factors other than rising damp caused by moisture in the ground, eg leaking gutters or downpipes, defective drains, open joints or cracks in walls, moisture tapped behind hard renders, burst plumbing, condensation due to inadequate ventilation, etc. If, however, rising damp is diagnosed, the measures taken to reduce it will vary according to particular conditions.

Where the external ground level is higher than the floor level, causing moisture to penetrate horizontally through the wall, the possibility of regrading the ground levels should first be investigated. If this is not feasible, then an open trench or 'dry area' may be formed with a French drain at its base.

Provided the foundations are not too shallow, this method may also be used when the external ground level is not higher than floor level but where a high water table is causing rising damp. In these circumstances, however, a more economical solution is to install a simple French drain without a 'dry area'. A drain should be kept at least 200mm from a foundation base. Before embarking on excavation adjacent to an historic building, however, archaeological advice should be obtained and, where appropriate, supervision and recording by a specialist should be arranged.

Where it is not feasible to provide perimeter drainage, the following methods may be considered.

Fig 34   Salt crystallisation damage to brickwork caused by rainwater splashing up from the hard perimeter surface

- The insertion of a damp-proof membrane by cutting a slot in short lengths across the full width of the wall and inserting a strip of material such as lead, lead-cored bitumen felt, copper, heavy-gauge polythene, etc. Each length of membrane must have an adequate lap over or below its neighbour. This method is restricted, however, to walls of regular-coursed masonry, of a thickness not too great for the cutting machine, and the membrane must be inserted below the level of a timber ground floor.
- The formation of a damp-proof barrier by impregnating the masonry with a chemical solution. This method is unlikely to be effective when walls have rubble cores containing voids, unless these can be effectively consolidated prior to impregnation, or where walls are more than 600mm thick.

Measures such as the application of an impervious render or other waterproofed surface on the inside face should not be used, as they will only serve to trap moisture behind them and drive it further up the wall to emerge at a higher level.

Floors

A good thickness of hand-packed hardcore blinded off with fine material will provide a satisfactory base of bedding flagstones that will reduce rising dampness and not drive moisture elsewhere. Where rising damp and resultant salt deposits are significantly damaging a tiled or flagged ground floor, the insertion of a damp-proof membrane under the floor should only be considered where it is not possible significantly to improve the situation by installing perimeter drainage outside the building. Another method may be to form a gap between the edge of the floor and the wall to encourage evaporation of moisture. If such methods are not feasible and it is agreed that a membrane is needed, a damp-proofing system should be installed within the walls at the same time as the installation of the floor membrane, otherwise damp will be driven up the walls.

Membranes may be installed below the plates of timber ground-floor constructions when damp conditions exist. Voids below timber floors must be properly ventilated so that moisture may disperse.

In any disturbance of historic floors and their substrates, archaeological advice should be obtained and followed.

Repair of structural timbers
(Roof structures, wall frames, floor beams, etc)

Fungal attack

Outbreaks of fungal attack in timber (wet and dry rot) should be dealt with by identifying and remedying the cause; treatment with even the most potent fungicide will be ineffective if the source of moisture is not stopped (eg leaking gutters and downpipes, blocked parapet and valley gutters, blocked drains, etc) and proper permanent ventilation introduced to floor voids, roof spaces, partition studding, etc.

A fungicide-containing barrier may need

to be considered to prevent the spread of the fungus for as long as it takes for the affected part of the structure to dry out. The fungus will die off completely in dry conditions (ie below 20% moisture content) within about 12 months, although where timbers are embedded in thick masonry, it may take longer. During this time environmental conditions must be regularly and frequently monitored and controlled. It is only necessary to cut out and replace members or parts of members which are directly infected or structurally weakened by the fungus. The often destructive results of standard methods of eradication can thus be avoided.

Where fungal attack is discovered, particularly dry rot, measures should be taken against it immediately. Failure to do so in warm and damp conditions will risk its spreading rapidly. Ventilation is the most important immediate action, followed by the removal of any impervious finishes which prevent moisture dispersal.

Insect attack

Death-watch, common furniture beetle, and, more rarely, powder-post and house longhorn are the types of insect which cause structural damage. Careful investigation may be necessary in order to determine the severity of the attack and the extent to which the strength of a member has been impaired. This should, however, be carried out with great care on historic timbers and in the case of moulded work should be avoided in favour of treating and conserving the weakened timber surface. A drawn record should be made of the original timber profiles.

Before chemical timber treatment against wood-boring insects is considered it should be noted that such treatment is essentially a device to buy time, although it is likely to provide protection for approximately five years.

It is not necessarily appropriate to carry out chemical treatment simply as a 'precaution'; there should be clear evidence of need. Selective rather than wholesale treatment is always preferable.

Insecticide should be applied to all accessible surfaces by spray, brush, or injection, as appropriate, with particular attention to joints, shakes, and end grain. If preservative fluids are used they should only be of a water-based and colourless type and care should be taken to ensure that historic surfaces and decorative treatments are not damaged.

Where timbers are of large section and penetration is unlikely to be sufficient, the use of a paste may be preferable.

Where bats are inhabiting a building, treatments should be non-toxic to them. Under the Wildlife and Countryside Act 1981 there is an obligation to owners of such buildings to consult English Nature before any work is carried out.

Repairs

For the repair of a timber-frame building, survey drawings should be prepared for each wall, floor, and roof frame in its existing state, followed by drawings showing the repairs as proposed.

Wherever possible, repairs to structural timbers should be carried out in timber using traditional carpentry methods, retaining all sound existing material, and replacing only what is necessary in order to restore the structural integrity of the frame. Badly decayed or seriously split members or

parts of members should be carefully cut away and new sections spliced in, using timber of the same species and scantling as the original. Oak used in repairs should preferably be new, after a sufficient laying-down. The use of oak cannibalised from old buildings should be avoided.

Typical methods of repair are the use of scissor scarfs for main posts, bridle scarfs for horizontal members such as sole plates, shouldered scarfs where horizontal members are subject to bending stresses, and halved scarfs for the repair of vertical members such

Fig 36 A scissor scarf used to replace the decayed lower part of an oak corner post. The cause of decay was a long-standing leak from a defective cast-iron downpipe, now replaced

Fig 35 Major structural repair to a timber wall frame using traditional carpentry methods

Typical joints used in carpentry repairs

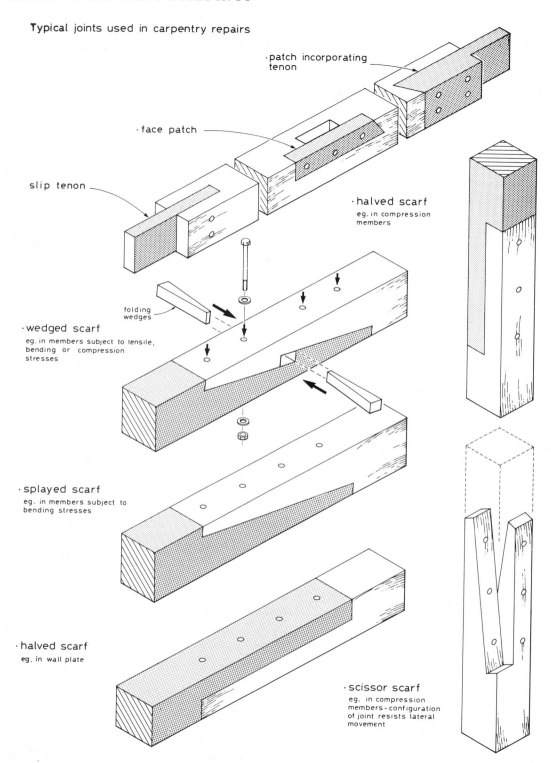

·patch incorporating tenon

·face patch

slip tenon

·halved scarf
eg. in compression members

folding wedges

·wedged scarf
eg. in members subject to tensile, bending or compression stresses

·splayed scarf
eg. in members subject to bending stresses

·halved scarf
eg. in wall plate

·scissor scarf
eg. in compression members – configuration of joint resists lateral movement

Fig 37 Scarf joints in traditional timber-to-timber carpentry repairs. In the situations exampled, these types of repairs should always be considered first, rather than resorting to substitute materials (illustration: Gower Technical Press)

as studs and slip tenons. It is particularly important that joints should function properly if the integrity of a structure is to be maintained.

If old timbers are found to have painted decoration which may be of interest, the advice of a specialist conservator and of English Heritage should be sought.

Oak pegs should not be replaced with steel bolts as this very considerably reduces the strength of a joint.

The repair of a weakened structure may sometimes be achieved by reinstating a missing member such as a brace or strut, or by making good a member cut through during alterations, eg a severed collar of a truss or a purlin severed when an attic was formed or a dormer window inserted.

Care should be taken when repairing a timber frame not to cause unnecessary damage to infill panels, which should be retained and repaired *in situ* whenever possible.

Although the carrying out of repairs by carpentry methods is usually to be preferred, these may sometimes involve undue disturbance of an historic structure. It may then be necessary to consider other methods, provided they are visually acceptable, eg a steel flitch or bolted plates or angles. Another method which occasionally may be appropriate is the use of carbon fibre reinforcement rods to carry out the *in situ* strengthening of a decayed structural

Fig 38   *In situ scarfed repairs and face patches to an oak wall frame*

member. After the rods are inserted they may be secured in place with resin and their ends concealed with a plug of matching timber.

In some cases strengthening may be achieved by the insertion of additional timber members alongside existing ones, such as the duplication of rafters or perhaps the insertion of an intermediated truss where a roof is not exposed internally. Care should be taken, however, not to introduce too many changes in load patterns, as they can trigger off new problems.

The use of resins in timber repairs should only be considered with great care and only normally where carpentry methods are

Fig 39   *New ends in oak scarfed on to decayed rafters (photo Leeds City Council)*

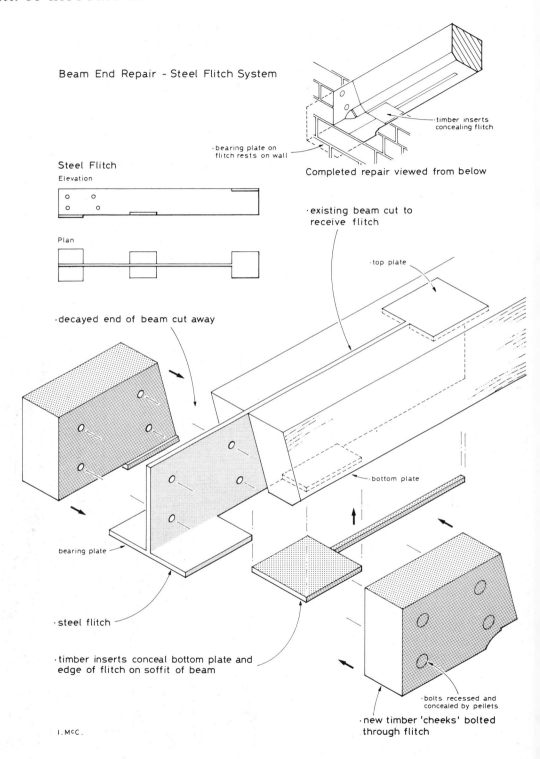

Beam End Repair - Steel Flitch System

Steel Flitch

Elevation

Plan

·bearing plate on
 flitch rests on wall

·timber inserts
 concealing flitch

Completed repair viewed from below

·existing beam cut to
 receive flitch

·top plate

·decayed end of beam cut away

·bottom plate

bearing plate

·steel flitch

·timber inserts conceal bottom plate and
 edge of flitch on soffit of beam

·bolts recessed and
 concealed by pellets

·new timber 'cheeks' bolted
 through flitch

I.McC.

*Fig 40   Beam end repair using a stainless steel flitch plate. The plate sits in the pit-sawn slot shown in preparation on page 17.
The steel is completely concealed, on completion of the repair, by oak cheeks and inserts (illustration: Gower Technical Press)*

impracticable. They should not be used where timbers are exposed to external conditions. On no account should they be looked upon as an 'easy option'. In cases where it is agreed that their use is appropriate, the work should always be carried out by a carpenter experienced in the repair of historic buildings and with an understanding of how they function structurally.

In some circumstances epoxy resins may enable *in situ* repairs to be carried out involving minimal loss of historic fabric, eg where there are voids formed by insect attack behind an original moulded or carved face of a member which it is of prime importance to preserve. In such conditions, wood consolidants may also be considered to help conserve friable carved work. Care should be taken not to solidify joints with epoxy resin as this will prevent the structure from adjusting itself freely in response to stresses.

Where there are shakes or other crevices in externally exposed timbers they should not be filled for cosmetic reasons, but should be filled if they are allowing water to enter and be retained, thus causing decay. Pegged patch repairs in matching timber should be used for larger defects. A suitable filler may be considered for smaller voids but it must be sufficiently flexible, and must be unlikely to shrink, as this would allow water to enter and be trapped, causing more decay than if nothing had been done. Only part-filling is normally necessary.

Apart from colourless preservatives, surface treatment or colour should not be applied externally to a timber frame unless it is intended to follow an existing historic treatment, eg 'brushed off' limewashing or 'black and white'. In the case of 'black and white', tar should not be used as this will prevent the timber from breathing naturally and cause it to rot. A suitable stain should be used instead.

The cleaning of a timber frame should be considered only with extreme caution and is only likely to be appropriate in exceptional circumstances. Even when carefully carried out, a method such as sandblasting will almost certainly detrimentally alter the surface texture of timber and carries the risk of removing surviving painted decoration or other evidence of a building's history.

Repair of stonework

Where dirt deposits on stonework or brickwork are of a kind that is actually causing damage, eg blistering sulphate skins on limestone or where they are of such thickness that it is not possible to decide properly on the scope of necessary repairs, then their removal is desirable. Very careful cleaning by a specialist conservator is usually an essential preliminary to conservation work on valuable carved work, etc. Unless there are such sound practical reasons, however, the cleaning of masonry is best avoided because of the damage which may be caused, and in some cases listed building

Fig 41 The blackening of this stonework is not likely to be causing damage and its removal for cosmetic reasons should be avoided

consent will be required for cleaning. If it is decided that cleaning is necessary, the method to be used will depend on the nature of the soiling and the type of stone or brick. Some methods, eg grit-blasting, should be avoided in almost all circumstances and always on brickwork. When a technique, or, if appropriate, a combination of techniques, has been selected and agreed, a sample of cleaning should be approved by the architect before work proceeds.

It is essential that the causes of damage and decay of stonework are first carefully investigated and identified in order that, where possible, their effect may be eliminated or reduced and decisions on the scope and methods of repair may be correctly related to them.

Typical problems are repeated crystallisation of salts within the pores or on the surface of the stone, acidic rainfall, run-off from lichens, splitting due to the freezing of water in pockets or crevices, the weathering out of soft clayey or sandy beds, contour scaling of sandstone, wrongly bedded stonework, serious rising damp, decay caused by insufficient protection of surfaces due to damaged drip-moulds, copings, etc, leaking gutters or downpipes, spalling caused by expansion of rusting iron cramps or window ferramenta, sandstone decayed by run-off from limestone, defective pointing, inappropriate or aggressively executed cleaning, stone decay caused by

Fig 42 The expansion of rusting window ferramenta causing stonework to spall. The ends of the ferramenta should be tipped with a suitable non-ferrous metal and the stone repaired by piecing-in

Fig 43 Careful and conservative repair of limestone, replacing only those stones which were decayed in depth, together with the hoodmould of the window, to allow it to perform its weathering function

hard, cement-rich mortars for pointing, areas of surface spalling due to trapped moisture caused by inappropriate attempts to preserve the stone, such as the application of silicone, linseed oil, etc, or damage by masonry bees.

Stones should only be replaced where they have lost their structural integrity because of deep erosion, or serious fracture or spalling, or where weatherings are no longer performing the function of throwing water clear of surfaces below. If erosion or spalling is only superficial it should be accepted, and loose, water-holding material lightly and carefully brushed off. The redressing of surfaces is not appropriate in most cases.

Decisions on the extent of replacement should, however, also take account of practical considerations. Difficulty of access and the cost of scaffolding, eg when working on towers, clerestories, etc, may make it suitable to carry out all work that is likely to be necessary for, say, the next 25 years. Also, the 'design intent' may be a factor to be taken into account, while working within the guiding principle of conserving as much of the existing fabric as possible.

The scope of replacement should be agreed as far as possible from the ground and from ladders, etc, prior to the preparation of a specification and schedule. The schedule should include marked-up photocopies of sufficiently detailed photographs, or be shown on drawings. Areas for repointing, any cracks to be stitched, or zones to be grouted, etc should also be indicated.

When scaffolding has been erected (which should have plastic pole end caps for the protection of the stone), the stonework should be inspected in detail in order that the work may be agreed on a stone-by-stone basis and the schedule confirmed or amended as necessary. Stones should be marked on the building to correspond with those marked on photocopies or drawings.

For the repair of window tracery, the photocopies or drawings should differentiate between stones which require indents, those

which need to be cut out to the glass line only, and those needing replacement in full depth (comparatively rarely necessary).

Where it is agreed that a feature needs to be dismantled and rebuilt, such as a pinnacle, parapet, cupola, etc, all stones should be numbered, with corresponding numbers shown on a detailed drawing, in order to ensure accurate reinstatement.

If it is agreed that moulded or carved work needs to be replaced (*see below*), the details of the original should be matched as exactly as possible by measuring a sheltered,

Fig 44 Window dressings, etc, have been largely replaced in ashlar, the original, but surface decay on walling stonework has been aggressively tooled off, thus radically changing the appearance of the building

uneroded section or by referring to reliable documentation. Detailed drawings should be approved in advance. Replacement stones should match the original in size, shape, colour, texture, qualities of durability, and surface finish, eg rubble for rubble and ashlar for ashlar; any tooling must be carefully carried out to match a sheltered example of the original. It is also important to ensure that bed joints are correctly finished.

Ideally, stone should come from the same quarry as the original, provided the durability of the currently available stone is considered adequate and can be obtained in sufficient depth of bed. If this is impossible, a matching, geologically compatible stone should be obtained. In general, cast stone is inappropriate, and it has different weathering qualities from natural stone. Where, exceptionally, reconstituted stone has to be considered the original stone dust should be used if possible.

Generally, except when dealing with carved or moulded work or with window tracery, a number of small stone indents should be avoided, so that original joint-lines are respected. Another possible exception may be where relatively small spalls have occurred due to rusting iron cramps. After the removal of the cramp and its replacement in stainless steel or phosphor bronze, the stone may be repaired with a small indent, unobtrusively rubbed-in, or tooled to match its parent stone. Such indents should not cross existing joint-lines.

Fig 45 An ironstone wall into which stone of a different type has been crudely inserted straight from the saw

Replacement stones should normally be set to the original face-line, unless to do so would produce an unacceptably obtrusive effect, in which case some compromise may be justified. Replacement stones (when sedimentary rocks) should be correctly bedded, usually on their natural bedding plane, except for cornices, copings, string courses, etc, which should be edge-bedded, and arch voussoirs, which should be set approximately parallel to the radius of the arch.

Fig 46 The somewhat obtrusive use of small indents, the lower one not respecting the original joint lines

Carved work should, wherever possible, be conserved and consolidated rather than replaced, ie an attempt should be made to hold back or slow down the rate of decay. It is likely that a comprehensive programme of repair will involve a combination of conservation and consolidation in some areas and stone replacement in others.

Methods of conservation and consolidation which may be considered are as follows.

- Plastic or special mortar repair. This should only be used sparingly, in the spirit of 'dentistry', for the filling of relatively small cavities which may hold water. It should not be seen as an inexpensive alternative to necessary replacement. In fact, if properly carried out by a skilled mason/conservator, as it should be, it is rarely cheaper. Its principal merit is that it often allows for the retention of more of the original fabric than if stone were to be pieced-in, but it should never be used in lieu of essential structural repair
- The holding of valuable fractured stone by stainless steel pins set in a low-viscosity epoxy resin
- Prolonging the life of masonry attacked by salts by, in the case of limestones, attempting to remove the salt with a poultice or a 'sacrificial' render of lime and sand, or, in some circumstances, lime putty
- Consolidation of limestone by the 'lime method' of repeated applications of limewater, the filling of cracks and small cavities with special repair mortar, and the provision of a sacrificial lime 'shelter coat'
- The use of alkoxy silane-based consolidants with the object of arresting the rapid loss of friable material from valuable stonework. It is claimed that this treatment achieves a deep penetration (over 20mm) which lines the pores of the stone, while allowing it to continue to 'breathe'. This method should only usually be considered, however, where other measures are unlikely to be effective, largely because its long-term effects are as yet uncertain. It is also expensive. The advice of an expert stone conservator should first be obtained and the consolidant should only be applied by specialists in strict accordance with supplier's instructions. It should not be used where rising damp and the presence of salts are a continuing problem

- The provision of lead flashings to prolong the life of decayed projecting features, including cornices, but only where this can be achieved unobtrusively

For important carved work, the carrying out of any of the above measures should be preceded by the creation of a full drawn and photographic record for future reference, when replacement may ultimately become unavoidable, before the stage where the erosion is such that a carving loses its architectural and artistic value. The point at which a decision needs to be made to consider the removal of original work and place it under cover for protection, replacing it with a copy, is not usually easy to determine. The advice of a specialist conservator and of English Heritage should be obtained.

In cases where a type of stone is of very poor weathering quality, either inherently so or because of poor selection, and where long

Fig 47 Limewater consolidation and shelter coating will prolong the life of this fifteenth-century doorway

exposure has resulted in an overall extremely severe degree of decay, it may in exceptional circumstances be appropriate to consider rendering, if the only alternative would be to reface completely. Such an alteration would clearly have a major effect on the character of a building and would require listed building consent. Rendering would rarely if ever be an acceptable option for a badly decayed building of fine architectural quality

Fig 48 Well-repaired flint rubble work

in ashlar. Other considerations are whether or not the depth of decay in the stone is endangering the structure and whether or not the stone is capable of allowing render properly to adhere to it. Where appropriate, specialist advice should be sought at an early stage (see *Repair of external render* for advice on render).

The repair of flint masonry presents different problems from those normally encountered. The material itself is virtually indestructible, but because of its smoothness and impermeability, and because of the smallness of the units, it is difficult to achieve a satisfactory bonding. There is a tendency for facework to part from its backing, particularly if water is allowed to enter through defective joints and then to freeze. In rubble flintwork joints should, therefore, be kept properly filled because when they fail, and flints begin to fall out, general deterioration can be fairly rapid. Finely jointed knapped and squared flintwork is much less vulnerable but can fail if water enters the core and washes mortar away. In such cases grouting of the core may be required.

Repair of brickwork

Many of the considerations which apply to the repair of stonework also apply to brickwork, and again the causes of decay should first be identified and wherever possible remedial measures taken to prevent or reduce further damage.

As with stonework, damage is most frequently the result of water penetration, so exposed features such as cornices, string courses, copings, plinth offsets, etc are likely to be most affected, particularly where formed of the soft bricks known as rubbers used in gauged work. Open joints and cracks will of course accentuate water penetration.

Rising damp often brings with it damage from salt crystallisation and the softer types of brick are the most likely to be affected.

Where a wall is exposed on both sides (eg a parapet) and is therefore more vulnerable to saturation, it is very likely that frost damage may occur. In some cases it may be advisable to consider protecting the inside face of a parapet, eg with render, tile, slate, or lead cladding.

Where individual defective bricks are found in an otherwise sound area of wall this is often the result of poor firing or because of 'foreign' material in the clay.

The number of bricks that are sufficiently decayed to be in need of replacement should be accurately identified. Only bricks that are beyond retention on structural grounds should be renewed. This is particularly important in the case of early brickwork or fine-quality gauged work, repairs to which should be recorded on marked-up drawings.

The method of cutting out should be chosen so as to cause the minimum of disturbance to surrounding sound bricks. In some cases, where an excessive degree of disturbance is likely to be caused, it may be necessary to use brick slips rather than full-depth bricks, but this method should be restricted to individual bricks or very small areas because of inherent structural weakness.

Replacement bricks should match the existing ones in dimensions, strength and durability, texture of finish, and colour. They should be laid in the same bond and width of joint. It is particularly important in achieving the latter to ensure that an exactly matching size of brick is selected. The appearance of a wall can be seriously impaired by different joint widths for areas of replacement brickwork.

In order to achieve a proper match it may be necessary to have new bricks specially fired, in which case the need to order sufficiently far in advance should be anticipated. Matching secondhand bricks may be available, although this source should be viewed with suspicion as it often entails damage to or loss of another historic building. Care should also be taken to ensure that secondhand bricks were not intended for internal use only and are therefore unable to withstand external weathering.

Where a wall or part of it is structurally unstable and rebuilding is unavoidable, a

Fig 49 This rusticated mid seventeenth-century archway, shown before recent repairs, had a number of deeply eroded bricks, but the extent of replacement needed to be very carefully considered to ensure that the character was not seriously impaired

record should be made prior to dismantling to ensure an accurate reconstruction. This is especially the case where brickwork incorporates decorative patterns such as diaper work.

In the case of early brickwork which may be in a generally fragile condition and where disturbance of the structure and loss of original fabric must be kept to the absolute minimum, it may be justifiable to carry out limited special mortar repairs (plastic

Fig 50 Bricks of the wrong type have been inserted into the façade of this fine early eighteenth-century house

repairs). These should be confined, however, to the filling of water-holding cavities, etc and not used as an alternative to necessary structural repair. Bricks should be dealt with individually and the plastic repair mortar not spread across the joint. The correct matching of colour and texture is difficult to achieve and even if initially successful may change later following exposure. Mixes incorporating sharp sand of the correct colour and brick dust should be used rather than resorting to the use of pigments.

Fig 51 Brickwork repairs of a suitable type in the process of being carried out to this late nineteenth-century chimneystack

Fig 52 Sound old pointing is an important part of the character of a building and should not be removed for unnecessary repointing

Repointing of stonework and brickwork

Repointing should only be undertaken where mortar has weathered out, leaving open or deeply recessed joints vulnerable to water penetration, or where the mortar is very soft or loose.

The comprehensive repointing of a building is rarely necessary. Those parts which are most exposed to the weather are most likely to be in need of attention, as are areas affected by specific problems such as rising damp. Even in such cases, deterioration may not be uniform and sound old pointing should be left undisturbed. Pointing is an essential part of the fabric and character of a building and its unnecessary removal is unacceptable.

Mortar should not be removed forcibly by the use of a mechanical disk or other unsuitable methods which are likely to cause damage to arrises or increase the width of joints.

Loose pointing should be carefully raked out manually, using a knife or spike. For the repointing of finely jointed work (which is rarely necessary), a hacksaw blade is a suitable tool for cleaning out the joint. Cutting out, using a sharp quirk and a small lump hammer, may be necessary where there is a hard, cement-rich mortar, usually dating from a previous repointing operation. Due to its impermeability this will cause stones or bricks to erode more rapidly than the joint itself. The removal of hard mortar should be carried out with great care, however, and should not be attempted if it will cause more damage to the fabric than if the hard mortar is left until it has loosened sufficiently to allow easier removal.

When repointing, a sound example of original pointing should, wherever possible, be found in a sheltered part of the building and carefully matched in mix and finish in the new work. In choosing an example to copy, however, care should be taken to ensure that it is not in fact inappropriate later work which is mistakenly selected.

In cases where it is impossible to copy an original mortar or the facilities for analysis

Fig 53 The forcible removal of mortar by the use of a mechanical cutter, thus widening the joints. The damage has been compounded when repointing by buttering the mortar beyond the joints on to the face of the bricks

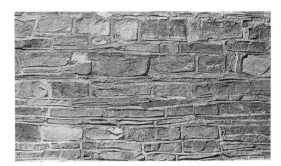

Fig 54 Unsuitably repointed sandstone rubble in a cement-rich mortar

are unavailable, a mix should be chosen which is compatible with the porosity and strength of the particular stones or bricks in a wall and suitable for the degree of exposure to the weather of a particular location. The general principle is that the mortar should be slightly weaker than the stone or brick. Mortar which is harder will prevent moisture from evaporating out through the joints so that instead it comes out only through the stones or bricks, increasing the rate of decay and leaving the hard mortar standing proud. For this reason the inclusion of any cement in a mix should wherever possible be avoided. Mixes will vary considerably according to circumstances (eg the stone or brick type), but a rough guide is a proportion of 1:3 of binding agent (lime) to aggregate (a sharp sand, well washed and graded). The strength of mix also needs to be related to the degree of exposure, eg parapets and chimneystacks usually require a relatively stronger mix than sheltered areas.

Additives and pigments should be avoided and the correct colour should be obtained by adjusting the aggregates, although care should be taken not to use too much stone or brick dust in a mix for this purpose as this can cause cracking of the mortar.

The mortar should be packed firmly into the joint using a pointing iron after all loose material has been flushed out and the joint wetted to avoid suction.

The joint should be finished in accordance with the original form where there is evidence of it. This is particularly applicable where joints are finished with a special treatment (provided this is original and not recent), eg an incised line in the centre of each joint, 'beak' pointing, tuck-pointed brickwork, flint galleting, etc or for

Fig 56 Great care has been taken to produce this example of 'strap' pointing, an entirely unsuitable method but one which is widespread throughout the country. Not only is it offensive in appearance but it causes the stonework to decay more rapidly

Fig 55 Special forms of pointing, as here tuck pointing, should be carefully reproduced when repointing becomes necessary

finely finished masonry with extremely narrow joints filled with screened lime putty, the repointing of the latter is rarely needed but if it is it requires the skilled use of a specialist technique.

For joints which are not specially treated, a flush finish, fractionally recessed, is usually appropriate. On no account should mortar be spread beyond the joint on to the face of stones or bricks.

Where arrises are decayed, the mortar should be set back to be within the joint width proper, so as to avoid feather edges, which will soon crack away allowing water penetration. In masonry which is not finely finished, eg wide-jointed brickwork, rubble stonework, random flint walling, etc it is appropriate to finish the joint by dabbing the mortar with a damp sponge or a bristle brush just after the initial set. Joints should *not* be smoothed off with a steel trowel.

Relatively recent forms of joint finish, such as 'strap' or 'ribbon' pointing raised above the surface, 'bucket-handle', 'weather-struck', etc, usually carried out in hard, cement-rich mortars, are quite unsuitable in historic buildings work. Inappropriate methods of repointing are among the most frequent causes of damage to the character of old buildings and also of damage to the masonry of which they are built.

A sample of pointing should always be approved by the architect before work proceeds.

Repair of chimneystacks

As exposed features of a building, chimneystacks are particularly vulnerable to decay, both from erosion of stonework or brickwork by the action of rain, wind, or frost and by chemical attack caused by sulphates in the flue gases. When sulphate gets into the joints, expansion of the mortar can create a wedging effect, causing general instability and often a leaning over of the stack, aided by the wetting and drying of the side of the stack exposed to the prevailing wind and rain. Internal inspection is strongly advised in such cases.

Fig 57 (above and below) *A fine medieval chimneystack shown before and after the careful repair and repointing of its rubble and dressed stonework*

Where decay is confined to individual stones or bricks these may be cut out and replaced to match, or where the erosion of mortar is not in full depth, repointing will suffice, but if a combination of the factors described above applies it will be necessary to dismantle a stack and rebuild. In this case a measured survey should be carried out and the sound units numbered in order to facilitate an accurate reconstruction.

In the case of early stacks, particularly brick ones, and where there is not a serious lean, it is preferable to consider stabilisation *in situ* to avoid the risk of an unacceptable degree of damage to original fabric which dismantling may cause. Where the existing flue is wide and straight enough, this may be done by inserting a pipe of stainless steel, with a gap of at least 100mm between it and the inner face of the original flue, so that this may act as both a flue liner and as

permanent shuttering to a reinforced concrete lining to the stack. It is important to ensure that a flue remains open in order to maintain ventilation.

Where a chimneystack which is important to the design of a building has earlier been reduced in height it should be reinstated in its original form, provided evidence for this exists. Proposals for removing a chimneystack will not normally be acceptable, except where it is agreed to be an intrusive later addition and is in poor conditions. Listed building consent will be required.

Badly damaged or missing chimneypots should be reinstated to the original pattern. If fractured, valuable early ceramic pots or fine decorative ones of a later date should be repaired by 'stitching' across the fracture. This work should be carried out by a specialist.

Repair of terracotta and faience

An early use of terracotta was in the sixteenth century for a limited number of relatively important buildings. Surviving examples are rare and deserve the greatest possible degree of care in their conservation, with the object of retaining the maximum amount of existing material. Such work should only be carried out by specialist conservators. Techniques may include the consolidation of an eroding underbody exposed by the loss of the fireskin, possibly using an alkoxy silane, although this should be approached with caution, the careful filling of small voids with special mortars, the withdrawal of rusting iron fixings and replacement with non-ferrous material, and the protection of vulnerable projecting features with lead flashings unobtrusively placed, etc.

Coade Stone, a patent form of terracotta, appeared in the late eighteenth century and was used in refined decorative work, often with the intention of simulating stone. The most widespread use of terracotta was, however, from about the end of the first quarter of the nineteenth century until the second decade of the twentieth, although thin faience cladding continued to be

Fig 58 Before and after the authentic replacement in terracotta of important features

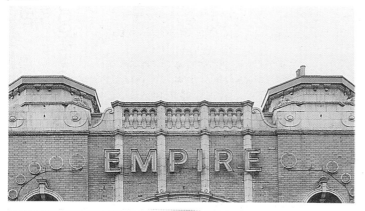

popular for buildings such as cinemas, hotels, shops, etc in the 1920s and '30s.

Terracotta usually performs well if water can be prevented from penetrating. This can occur if, due to defective firing, there are faults in glazing or in the hard fireskin, which, once breached, can lead to the rapid deterioration of the weaker underbody due to frost action or the crystallization of soluble salts. Glazing of the fireskin can also be damaged by aggressive cleaning using acid.

In addition, water may enter via cracks caused by stress, resulting from differential movement between the terracotta blocks and the back-up structure. Water penetration may also occur via hairline cracks in the mortar between blocks which was often originally of too hard a mix to allow for flexibility of movement or to allow moisture to evaporate once it had entered.

One of the most serious results of water penetration is the rusting of iron or steel members used to fix the terracotta to the underlying structure. Unless there are tell-tale stains or spalling of the arrises, such damage may not be apparent from the ground and may only come to light when its effects are far advanced, causing major cracking and loosening of units. Non-destructive techniques of investigation will be of considerable use in identifying such problems when they are more fully developed.

Rusted fixings which are causing structural failure should be dealt with by carefully removing the terracotta units and, where possible, completely de-rusting and treating the fixings. Where corrosion is very severe, however, it will be necessary to replace the fixings in stainless steel or non-ferrous metal. Broken units of terracotta may be repaired by dowelling and bonding with epoxy resin.

Where replacement blocks are needed these can be obtained from one of a small number of manufacturers still in operation. They should match the existing ones in quality, size, colour, and finish. GRP should not be used as an alternative.

Where it appears that corroded fixings are not a problem, *in situ* repairs may be carried

Fig 59   Repair of an individual block of terracotta using a special mortar, which does not achieve a satisfactory match. Note the damage to the surface of the original terracotta caused by acid cleaning

out by grouting voids behind blocks with low-viscosity resin and by refixing loose blocks by drilling and anchoring them with small-diameter stainless steel ties.

The repointing of defective joints should be carried out with a mortar mix which is weaker than the units themselves to allow for the evaporation of moisture through the joint, but particular care should be taken to ensure that the joints are solidly filled.

Small-scale repairs to individual blocks may be carried out with a special mortar to match the terracotta, using techniques similar to those for plastic repairs to stonework and brickwork, and taking care to avoid feather-edging. Colour matching of such special mortars should be achieved by choice of aggregate, not the use of pigments which usually leach out in time, causing the repair to appear unsightly.

Large-scale plastic repairs are not appropriate, nor is the facing-up of damaged terracotta with mortar followed by overall painting. This will completely change the character of the building.

Repair of external render

There are many types of external render, characteristic of different periods and regions and applied for different reasons to various kinds of backing material. Each type, and its particular finish and associated details, is usually an essential part of the original character of the building to which it is applied, or part of a significant later remodelling which gives the building its present character. It is important that this character is not damaged by inappropriate methods of repair and materials, and analysis of the existing render should be a prerequisite of repair.

Render should not be removed in order to expose, eg, rubble stonework or timber framing, which were not intended to be exposed, nor should it be removed where there are good reasons for render having been applied at a later date.

Medium to low-strength lime-based renders

These are either flat-finished or textured (the latter variously known as rough-cast, wet-dash, or harling), or they allow parts of stones to show through. They are intended to act as a protective outer layer to a building. Periodically, they require extensive repair or replacement, the frequency of which largely depends on the degree of exposure.

To function correctly, the render must be no stronger than the material to which it is applied in order to be sufficiently flexible to accommodate movement and to allow moisture to evaporate freely from it. Hard, cement-rich mixes should not be used to replace such lime-based renders as their lack of flexibility will cause them to crack, allowing water to penetrate and be trapped, eventually leading to the failure of the render and the decay of the masonry itself.

Wherever possible an existing render should be analysed so that the mix may be copied, and a sheltered area should be examined in order to determine the original colour and texture of the finish. The latter should be achieved by the choice of aggregates. Pigments should be avoided, except where the use of natural earth pigments is appropriate. As a rough guide a typical mix might be 1:3 (lime putty : sharp sand) for laying-on coats (about three coats), and 3:5:6 (lime putty : sharp sand : pea

Fig 60   The render had been removed from this rubble stone wall with the misguided intention of leaving the stonework exposed after pointing, but it was clear that this was never originally intended and the render has now been replaced

with the object of simulating expensive ashlar. They were capable of incorporating the full range of architectural features usually associated with masonry. Wall surfaces are often channelled to give an appearance of rustication or lined-out in imitation of finely jointed work.

From the mid eighteenth century oil mastic stuccos were produced and in 1794 Parker's Roman Cement was patented, a quick-setting natural hydraulic cement which was widely used throughout the nineteenth century. It is characteristically a buff colour, and was often finished by a wash of lime and copperas.

In the mid nineteenth century artificial cements were developed by firing together a combination of ground limestone and clay, called Portland Cement. When mixed with sand or lime and sand these cements produced renders of high strength and impermeability.

Fig 61   Good practice in rough-cast lime render, coated with limewash

gravel) as a finishing coat suitable for rough-cast. It is, however, impossible to generalise and mixes will vary from area to area and according to building type and period. Bonding agents should be avoided. The wall should be wetted before the application of the render in order to reduce suction.

Where a rough-cast rendered wall has an undulating surface, eg a rubble stone wall, this should be accepted and no attempt made to face it up with the render for the sake of providing a flat finish.

The existing details at openings, corners, etc should be followed.

The render may be left uncoated if finished with limewash, if appropriate, but on no account should an impermeable paint system be used as this will lead to the entrapment of moisture.

Smooth renders or stuccos

These were most often applied to brickwork, although occasionally to rubble stone, often

Fig 62   Major failure of dense, impervious render on limestone following cracking, aided by the friable surface of the limestone itself

Failure of these high-strength stuccos is usually caused by water penetration through cracks or by defects resulting from lack of maintenance, leading to loss of adhesion. Surface deterioration may be caused by the crystallisation of soluble salts.

Defective stucco should be cut out in areas clearly defined by architectural features or by the corners of a facade, so as to avoid a patchy appearance resulting from a contrast between new and existing work. A proper key should be provided by ranking out joints in the masonry and by undercutting adjacent existing stucco which is to be retained. Mixes and surface finishes and colour should be carefully matched to the existing work, although as Roman Cement is no longer made it is necessary to use other means to achieve a similar result, eg a plasticised cement mixed with red and yellow sands, or, less satisfactorily, the use of pigments in cement or lime.

Suitable mixes for repairing oil mastics, Roman Cements, or Portland Cement renders are 1:1:6 (cement:lime:sand) for backing coats and 1:2:9 for a top coat.

Non-traditional features such as bell drips, metal angles, and stops, etc should be avoided.

All architectural details such as rustication, lining-out, balustrades, cornices, orders, architraves, etc must be carefully copied in repairs. Where such details have been previously hacked off and patched over they should be accurately reinstated in accordance with adjacent existing work or old photographs. Detailed drawings should be prepared.

Where stucco is painted, the existing type of paint should be used provided this is suitable, eg a lime-casein mix or an oil-bound distemper, etc. Modern impervious paint systems which are intended to provide a 'waterproof' coating to a building should

Fig 63   Roman Cement was used for the main elements of this late eighteenth-century façade (the capitals, swags, statues, and urns are in Coade Stone). Cracks along the soffit of the entablature will increase with further water penetration. Great care will be necessary to achieve a suitable mix to match the Roman Cement

not be used as they will trap moisture behind them and cause deterioration of the stucco. Paint finishes which alter the texture of the existing finish are also unacceptable.

Repair of infill panels in timber-framed buildings

Where wattle and daub infill panels survive they should be retained and carefully repaired as necessary. The panel construction of riven oak staves, around which are woven either hazel withies or riven oak laths, may be affected by rot and beetle attack and be in need of preservative treatment and repair or partial replacement. If beetle attack is no longer active it can be ignored if it does not affect the stability of a panel. When daub has decayed, usually because of lack of maintenance of the limewashed outer face and resulting water penetration, it should be made good in a

Fig 64 Old infill panels in timber frames should be repaired using traditional techniques and replacing defective daub where required, not by introducing inappropriate materials such as woodwool, seen in the lower panel

matching mix, of which there are many traditional variations. A typical daub may include a soil containing silt and sand and a small proportion of clay, together with a small amount of dung for workability and some chopped straw or hair for reinforcement. All should be mixed as dry as possible. Lime may be included in some daubs.

After allowing three or four weeks for drying out, the panel should be coated with limewash, which normally will adequately fill any fine cracks that may have developed.

In non-residential buildings, in cases where panels are missing or where wattle and daub panels have later been replaced with an inappropriate modern material which has become defective, the wattle and daub should be reinstated. In residential buildings, however, it may be reasonable in such cases to use new, lightweight, composite panels incorporating insulation and finished with lime render. Panels should be carefully detailed to prevent the ingress of moisture at the edges and should allow for any shrinkage or movement of a repaired frame.

Sometimes brick was used as the original infill material. In other instances it may have been put in later as a replacement for decayed wattle and daub and should normally be retained. Occasionally, however, there may be cases where the weight of the brickwork is threatening the stability of the frame and it may be wise to consider replacing it with a traditional wattle and daub panel or a lightweight panel finished with lime render, particularly where removal of the brickwork is in any case necessary in order to repair the frame itself. Statutory consent would be required for such a proposed alteration.

Repair of earth walls

The use of unbaked earth for the walls of vernacular buildings was an early form of construction. Its use was widespread in areas where the soil contained clay or chalk until around the mid nineteenth century when bricks became readily available.

Methods of construction and the names given to them vary according to the areas in

Fig 65 Major failure at the gable end of this earth-walled building due to water penetration from the defective eaves and through cracks in cement render which has then prevented drying out. Methods of repair which may be considered are suttering on both sides and building up between with a matching mix, or inserting pre-made blocks made from a matching mix

or brick plinth to prevent rising damp or damage by rain splash. Surface protection is often provided by limewashed earth or lime renders. The proper maintenance of these elements is essential if rapid deterioration is to be avoided. It is essential that the structure is able to breathe; impervious paint finishes or hard impervious surface render should never be used.

Regional types

West country earth-walling is known as cob. In the area from Cornwall to Hampshire the constituents are generally clayey and sandy sub-soils and straw. The walls are built without shuttering, usually in lifts of approximately 600mm; they are trodden down and left to dry before the next lift. In parts of Hampshire and Wiltshire, pulverised chalk is used as the base of the mix while in parts of Buckinghamshire, a chalky clay is used, and here the form is known as wichert. In Northamptonshire the local ironstone clay is sometimes stable enough for straw to be omitted. In the Solway Plain clay is the main ingredient of the local form of earth wall, with straw chopped up in the mix. In parts of East Anglia, particularly in Norfolk, earth walls were later built of blocks of clay made in wooden moulds, a form of construction known as clay lump.

Pise, a French method, was introduced into the south of England in the late eighteenth century and is formed of semi-dry rammed earth built up between lifts of shuttering, enabling a greater degree of compaction and a more precise construction to be achieved.

Repairs

Each of the above regional types, and some others not mentioned, have their own particular characteristics which should be carefully respected and followed when making repairs. Unfortunately unsympathetic methods of repair are common, eg patching decayed areas with cement-rich mortars or filling holes with concrete blocks or bricks. These

which they were traditionally used, and in these areas surviving examples may be seen, although sometimes now obscured by a later covering such as brick. Generally, however, earth buildings are relatively rare and their loss in some areas (eg the Solway Plain, Cumbria) is of particular concern. It is important, therefore, that the buildings which do remain are retained and that when repairs are needed they are carried out in an appropriate manner with the correct materials.

Water penetration is the chief cause of decay in earth walls, so they were traditionally protected at the head by overhanging eaves and at the base by a stone

incompatible materials can cause damage to adjacent parts of the original structure and are to be avoided.

A particular problem associated with the repair of earth walls is the need to achieve sufficient compaction and to minimise drying-out and shrinkage so that the repair is compatible with the original work. Surface repairs and their key with the old material may be achieved by cutting back the area to be repaired so that it is undercut at the edges, and the existing surfaces are then wetted with a mist spray to achieve integration with the newly applied material which should be mixed to a stiff consistency.

It is important that any material used in these repairs is as close a match as possible with the original to ensure compatibility and integration with the old base. Reconstituted old material is the most likely to achieve compatibility but if this is not available an analysis of the old material should be made in order to achieve as close a mix as possible.

Compression of the new material behind a shutter board can provide good compaction but it must be appreciated that although a surface repair may maintain integrity with the old material it is unlikely to achieve the original strength.

Tapered oak pegs may be driven into the old wall in order to help the key, provided the surface will accept them. Alternatively tile slips set into slots may be considered, although as tiles are an alien material they should be used with caution.

Deep deterioration of the wall will require removal of the whole thickness and its replacement by building up in layers either with or without shuttering, or, alternatively, the insertion of pre-made and already shrunk earth blocks of matching mix to the original construction, bonded together with earth mortar.

Where open fissures have occurred in the wall as a result of water penetration they will need to be filled and can be stitched in a variety of ways, depending upon the stability of the wall. The fissure will need to be cut out as for surface repairs. The source of water penetration should of course be removed.

Damp-proof courses should usually be avoided, but if as a result of serious rising damp, the introduction of a damp-proof course becomes necessary, it should be applied only within the stone base and never within the earth structure itself. Unreasonable dampness within the building is, however, likely to be caused by factors that can be solved in other ways, for instance the reduction of the external ground level, provision of drainage, etc.

Repair of reinforced concrete structures

In the late nineteenth century concrete was sometimes used as an unreinforced filling material between iron or rolled steel joists in floors and flat roofs, usually with clinker as a main ingredient of the aggregate.

If water is allowed to penetrate, eg through a defective asphalt roof finish, the clinker will expand and, because allowance was not usually made for movement, the resulting pressure can cause bulging and cracking in perimeter parapets, walls, etc. If diagnosed at an early enough stage, the problem may not be serious and the prevention of further water penetration by the repair of the roof finish, together with the pointing of any cracks which may have

Fig 66 Spalling of concrete caused by the rusting and expansion of reinforcement. Where spalling occurs the reinforcement should be exposed, de-rusted, and treated, and the concrete made good, possibly incorporating a polymer in the mix if the cover is inadequate

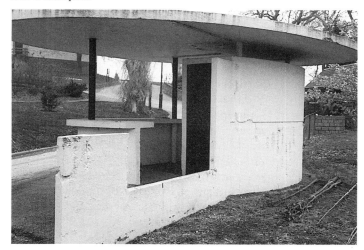

occurred in the masonry, may suffice. If allowed to continue unchecked, however, extensive structural repairs may be needed, possibly including the removal of the concrete in order to treat or replace rusted beams and the tying-in or partial rebuilding of distorted masonry.

In the early use of reinforced concrete it was not uncommon for inadequate or permeable cover to be given to the reinforcement, resulting in its corrosion and expansion and spalling of the concrete. Water may also enter because of the concrete becoming porous through leaching of soluble materials. In addition, chemical degradation of the concrete may occur from impurities contained in the sand or aggregate, or from additives introduced to increase workability.

Superficial methods of repair should be avoided, eg the surface spraying on of new concrete without dealing with underlying problems, such as rusted reinforcement. Such a method is also likely to be inappropriate because of the effect it may have on the appearance of the structure in altering the profile of members.

Where extreme degradation of elements of the structure has taken place, it may be necessary to dismantle and rebuild. New reinforcement should be given adequate cover and be well galvanised or epoxy-coated. Alternatively stainless steel may be used.

The majority or repairs, however, will involve the removal of cracked and spalled concrete in order to expose the reinforcement so that it may be completely de-rusted by chemical or mechanical means, followed by anti-corrosion treatment. Where the cover is adequate a new plain concrete mix may then be applied. Where the cover is not sufficient, however, a mix containing a polymer may be used, or possibly an epoxy resin mortar if strength is an important consideration. Permeability may also be reduced by sealing both the repaired and unrepaired areas.

Work to reinforced concrete should not usually be undertaken without the advice of a structural engineer.

Repair of ironwork

The nature of wrought iron
Wrought iron is produced by means of working pig iron (smelted iron ore) to remove virtually all carbon and other impurities, followed by further reheating and reworking to improve tensile strength.

From the fourteenth century, when the blast furnace was developed, until the eighteenth century, the use of wrought iron in buildings was largely confined to the ironmongery of doors, window ferramenta, straps, tie bars, and for gates and railings. By the end of the eighteenth century, technological improvements allowed for the manufacture of rolled sections which could be used structurally, and from the 1840s rolling machinery was introduced which speeded up production.

With the introduction of methods for producing mild steel in large quantities, first invented in 1856 and widely used by the 1880s, the labour-intensiveness and relatively high cost of wrought-iron production were much reduced. Today, however, apart from recycled material, new wrought iron is only available in small quantities.

Wrought iron has good tensile strength and when used structurally this quality was usually exploited, eg it was used for arched members of roofs and arcades, glazing bars particularly in curved roofs, and tie rods, etc. Wrought iron can be identified, where a fracture has occurred, by the fibrous nature of its internal structure, formed by beating or rolling. Characteristic structural details are jointing by forge welding, joints resembling timber methods, and the riveting of sections together to form composite members.

The nature of cast iron
Cast iron is made by pouring molten pig iron into moulds. Although poor in tension it is strong in compression. Structurally it is most suitable for columns, and when used for beams the bottom flanges need to be considerably thicker than for wrought-iron beams. Its uses for semi-structural and

decorative members are almost unlimited, eg brackets, staircases, railings and balustrades, roof ridges and finials, gutters and downpipes, etc. Cast iron can be identified where fractures have occurred by its relatively homogeneous, crystalline structure and by characteristic defects in castings such as blow holes. Further means of identification are slightly raised lines on the surface created by joints in moulds.

Corrosion

Both wrought and cast iron possess generally good anti-corrosion properties but where they are likely to be exposed to water and air it is essential that they are properly protected by a system of coatings of paint and that this is carefully maintained annually, especially in a marine environment. If unattended to, even small defects in coatings can allow water to enter, causing corrosion to develop underneath the coating, which will eventually blister off to reveal areas of rust.

On no account should rust be overpainted. Defective areas should be deal with by removing layers of paint and rust completely before priming and repainting. This may be done by methods such as simple scrapers, wire brushes, and sand papers, or by the use of roto-strippers or abrasive flap wheels, although these will not deal with detailed areas and should be used with care to avoid damage.

Where corrosion is extensive, often hidden under many layers of defective old paint which is also likely to clog up and obscure the detail of the ironwork, it is best that it is comprehensively removed.

Before this is done the paint layers should be analysed to enable an original colour scheme to be reinstated in appropriate cases.

Sandblasting is an effective method of cleaning for cast iron. If a building is in an area frequented by the public, however, the amount of gritty dust created by dry sandblasting is likely to be unacceptable, particularly if the paint is lead-based and, therefore, a health hazard. Wet-blasting, ie grit applied with a high-pressure water spray, or the use of a needle gun are preferable methods for *in situ*

Fig 67 Corrosion of cast-iron members caused by water penetration of a caviety

cleaning, although the latter should be used with care to avoid damaging the surface of the ironwork or of enrichment which may be of a different and softer material. Tannic acid-based rust converters can be used to neutralise rust or to treat delicate areas. Cleaning should be carried out as short a time as possible before the application of the first stage of the treatment process in order to prevent the development of rust.

The abrasive methods described above are not, however, to be recommended for the softer wrought iron. Flame cleaning, followed by the use of a wire brush, is the most suitable method, even though slower.

Fig 68 Air abrasive cleaning to remove paintwork from iron roof members to enable close examination of corroded joints

Where a structure can be dismantled, or where some dismantling is in any case necessary in order to remedy structural faults, cleaning may be carried out under more controlled conditions, possibly in a workshop. This will also allow for all-round treatment, particularly of joints. Before any dismantling is carried out, a structure should be recorded by means of drawings and photographs and each element numbered with a tag and on the drawing.

Structural repair

The removal or paint and rust may reveal further structural defects, both in the overall structure and in individual members, which were not apparent in an initial survey of their condition.

Movement may have taken place, possibly causing a redistribution of loads and the introduction of stresses in areas not originally designed to take them.

Engineering advice should be obtained to determine whether such stresses can be accepted without structural risk or whether action is needed. This may take the form of partial dismantling and re-erection, or the introduction of measures such as tie rods or additional elements for strengthening purposes such as plates (eg on the bottom flanges of beams), or even additional beams or columns. The latter may have the effect of radically changing the appearance of a structure and should only be considered as a last resort and subject to statutory consents.

Movement of the structure, either by load pattern behaviour or thermally, may cause members to fracture, particularly in the case of cast iron which is subject to tensile stress. Cast-iron columns may also fracture if they become filled with water which then freezes, either due to leaks or because they are intentionally designed to function as rainwater pipes, which may then have become blocked.

Fig 69 A plate repair to a cast-iron truss which, although structurally adequate, is not appropriate in terms of its appearance

Fig 70 A fracture in a cast-iron column repaired in situ by 'cold' metal stitching

In the latter case it may be possible to introduce a lining during repairs; alternatively, consideration may be given to the provision of separate downpipes, if this can be achieved unobtrusively. Fractures in cast iron my be repaired *in situ* by 'cold' metal stitching, which is both effective and unobtrusive.

Repair by welding is often very difficult to achieve successfully with cast iron, and then only usually for relatively small sections in workshop conditions. Welding is, however, an effective means of repairing broken sections of wrought iron or fixing on new pieces in place of corroded parts.

Where relatively small members are built into a wall (eg window ferramenta) and the end is badly corroded, it is sensible to fix a new tip in bronze or stainless steel rather than in iron, which may rust again in due course.

A structural repair may sometimes be achieved by reinstating a lost member, which should be copied from adjacent existing members. In the case of cast iron, patterns may be taken for a new casting to be made in an iron foundry, or, if dismantling of the structures has been necessary, an original section may be used as a pattern.

New castings should also be made of elements which are badly corroded beyond structural effectiveness and also of corroded or missing non-structural members which are important in the overall design.

Where it is necessary to replace wrought-iron members, recycled wrought iron should be used or new wrought iron obtained, if available.

Protective coatings

When de-rusting and the necessary repair or replacement of elements have been completed, ironwork should be fully and carefully protected by an appropriate system of coatings.

Before coatings are applied, any water-holding pockets as well as structurally non-significant but nevertheless defacing areas of corrosion may be made good by the use of metal fillers.

Immediately prior to treatment, the ironwork should be inspected for signs of rust which may have developed since the completion of de-rusting, particularly in conditions conducive to condensation. If any rust exists it should be removed by a flash flame clean, subject to necessary fire precautions being taken. On no account should coatings be applied in damp conditions.

The choice of a system of coatings will depend on such considerations as local environmental conditions, policy on maintenance, ease or difficulty of access, and the degree of historical interest of the structure or of any early paint which may remain. As an example, however, a system may comprise two priming coats of red lead or non-toxic zinc phosphate, then two coats of micaceous iron oxide, followed by two finishing coats of exterior-quality oil paint.

Repair of external and internal joinery

Joinery forming an integral part of a building may include such external features as cupolas, balustrades of roof platforms and balconies, ornamental bargeboards, eaves, cornices, windows and window surrounds, doors and doorcases, porches, etc, and such internal features as wall panelling, shutters, dados, skirtings, overmantels, doors together with architraves and overdoors, panelled ceilings, floorboarding, staircases and stair balustrades, etc. These will very often be essential elements in the original design of a building or of a significant later phase of alteration, and as such make a major contribution to a building's interest and importance. Details of joinery such as mouldings, carved decoration, etc are often valuable aids in indicating the date of a building or in identifying a craftsman or designer.

It is essential, therefore, in view of the relative vulnerability of joinery, particularly when external, to retain and preserve original material wherever possible by regular inspection and careful maintenance, and to carry out repairs when necessary using appropriate methods and materials.

Many of the considerations which apply to the repair of carpentry (see *Repair of structural timbers*) apply also to the repair of joinery. Damp penetration and fungus and insect attack are again the main agents of decay and their causes should be dealt with before repairs are carried out.

External joinery should be protected by regular painting. Lead weatherings on cornices, pediments of doorcases, etc should be properly maintained where they exist or introduced where appropriate, provided this can be done without adversely affecting the appearance of the feature or the building as a whole.

Voids formed within the carcassing of joinery, both external and internal, should be adequately ventilated to allow any moisture which may enter to evaporate readily before fungal growth can occur, and also to guard against conditions conducive to insect attack.

Joinery items much in use can be subject to considerable strain, leading to the loosening of joints and eventual fracture of sections, or to general collapse. To guard against this, such fittings as hinges on doors and casement windows, and cords and pulleys on sash windows should be kept in good order and replaced to match if broken beyond repair.

Much damage can be caused to internal joinery by the overheating of buildings, causing drying out of the timber followed by cracking and opening up of joints. Temperatures and humidity should be kept at a reasonable level and adequate general ventilation provided. Radiators, etc should be carefully sited so as to minimise damage.

The fundamental principle to adopt in repairing historic joinery is to replace only what is necessary, using timber of matching species and type of grain. Where new pieces are required they should be carefully jointed in, using the same technology as was used for the original in order to maintain the degree of flexibility necessary in features which are built up of many sections.

Although with carpentry it is possible to use unseasoned timber, joinery requires all timber to be fully seasoned. An important principle is that the moisture content of timber used in joinery repairs should match the old. This is necessary in order to avoid differential movement between old and new and consequential distortion, particularly in external work, and is also necessary where any adhesive has been used. In the worst cases, a new piece of unseasoned timber may eventually fall out, especially with repairs using very small slips of timber. These should in any case be used with caution as shrinkage cracks may form around them, allowing water to enter and cause decay.

It is often possible to dismantle part of a piece of joinery to facilitate the carrying out of a proper repair *in situ*. It is rarely necessary, therefore, to resort to alternative methods of repair, which should only be considered when *in situ* work is unavoidable. All joinery repairs should in any case be carried out by expert craftsmen, and this is an essential requirement where any dismantling is involved. Before any dismantling is carried out the positions of all existing members should be carefully recorded. Careless dismantling can cause considerable damage, particularly when timbers are decayed. This can often be the case when dismantling is carried out by other tradesmen in the course of their own work, eg the removal of skirtings or floorboards for the installation of heating pipes or electrical wiring. In such cases, damaged floorboards are frequently crudely replaced using softwood in place of elm or oak, and two narrow boards in place of an original wide one. When service installations affect historic joinery, an experienced joiner should be responsible for the careful lifting of boarding or removal of sections of wainscot, etc and for carrying out any

Fig 71 (above) and 72 (below) Conservative pieced-in repairs to eighteenth-century staircases

necessary repairs before reinstatement by splicing new pieces in matched timber. Splits should be repaired by gluing and clamping, with fixing blocks screwed on to the rear. When access to service runs is likely to be required regularly, floorboards should be discreetly fixed with screws in order to facilitate access and prevent damage.

It is particularly important when repairing moulded and carved joinery to ensure that the maximum amount of original material is retained. Where replacement is unavoidable, the new work should follow the existing work precisely, and where appropriate detailed drawings should be prepared and patterns made in advance. The work should be finished by hand; machine-run finishes should always be avoided.

The use of substitute materials such as GRP to simulate moulded or carved joinery is inappropriate.

Where a carved or moulded section of joinery survives intact only on its outer face, the bulk of the member behind it having decayed, it is important, if at all possible, that the authentic carving be retained *in situ*. In order to achieve this it may be necessary, following the removal of the decay, to refix the old work by means of adhesive to a new backing piece. Alternatively it may be possible, if the extent of decay is not general, to grout the voids with low-viscosity epoxy resin, but this method should be approached with caution and not used for external locations where moisture may become trapped behind the resin and thus accelerate decay.

Where valuable surfaces themselves are weakened by decay or insect attack, consideration may be given to strengthening them by impregnation with a consolidant such as an epoxy resin or an acrylic resin, which have different properties appropriate to particular conditions. Impregnation is achieved by a slow process of injection and must be entrusted to a specialist conservator.

When repairs are carried out to windows, only those sections which have decayed sufficiently seriously should be replaced; wholesale renewal for the sake of convenience should always be avoided. The profiles of decayed sections of glazing bars, etc, which need splicing should be copied exactly and be precisely married into the existing work. In the process of carrying out such work, all old glass should be carefully retained for reuse and not replaced with modern sheet glass.

When the complete replacement of a badly decayed window is necessary, the existing design should normally be reproduced exactly. On no account should an inappropriate modern replacement be substituted, even if superficially similar, eg a design intended to appear like a double-hung sash but in fact using top-hung lights. Substitute materials such as uPVC are equally completely inappropriate in an historic context.

Repairs may offer the opportunity for removing inappropriate or damaging later alterations and for reinstating an original design, provided that detailed evidence exists for this and subject to the necessary statutory consents. Caution should be exercised in considering such proposals, however, as alterations may contribute to the cumulative historic interest of a building, eg the insertion of nineteenth-century plate-glass sashes in place of small-paned sashes in a Georgian facade may be part of a significant phase of alteration to the building as a whole, or may possibly relate to a contemporary redesigning of the interiors.

Repair of glass
by Jill Kerr

Historically important glazing, whether painted, stained, or plain, is a job for a specialist conservator. As it requires considerable care to select the most appropriate workshop with the best stock, experience, and expertise to respond to particular problems presented by historical glass, both English Heritage and the Council for the Care of Churches may advise on the choice of conservator.

It is essential that the architect be fully involved with all aspects of the conservation,

Fig 73 The thick glazing bars of an early eighteenth-century sash window (right) and the thin ones typical of the late eighteenth century (left) illustrate the importance of accurate reproduction of details when carrying out repairs

Fig 74 Fixing with incompatible mortar applied without a specification drawn up by an architect which has, after two years, begun to crack and fail. In addition to the detrimental visual effect, the mortar also attaches a thin plastic cover, unventilated, which has no means of being removed without being chiselled from the mortar, canot flex, and which has already begun to attract superficial dirt (photo Jill Kerr)

preservation, repair, and reinstatement of historically important glazing. In particular, careful attention should always be paid to the following points of detail, which should be specified by the architect in sub-contracting to a glazier, mason, or iron or lead craftsman:

- the strength, texture, type, and tone of mortar to be used in the reglazing
- the method of fixing the glass – ensuring that ferramenta have non-ferrous tips, counter-sinking of iron in lead into masonry, the choice of joint for insertion of new tie bars, saddle bars, integral ironwork, and other holding devices – especially where the glass was originally glazed into a wooden frame rebated into stonework and retained by wooden pegs
- the preservation, reinstatement in working order, or, if necessary, redesigning of all ventilation required to maintain both control and regular passage of fresh air into the building
- the retention and careful conservation of all historically important window fixings, fitments, and ferramenta
- the careful recording *in situ* of all unusual fixing features before removing the glass; no historically important or interesting feature should be discarded or destroyed without full consultation or discussion, including, where appropriate, with English Heritage
- the careful retention and reuse of as much as possible of any original handmade glass, including old plain glazing, and of any other unusual features, such as horn or stretched oil cloth

Fig 75 (left) *wire netting within a metal frame inserted without any regard for the form of the window design;* (above) *wire guards laminated with protective plastic coating. These have been professionally designed and cut to follow the form of the tracery lights they protect. It is possible for a professional to design and shape wire guards to any architectural form and they should be finished in a colour to render hem as unobtrusive as possible* (photo *Jill Kerr*)

- the complete recording of any irregular or unusual leading patterns for plain glazing and all pictorial glazing by lead rubbing before dismantling the glass from the lead; the lead rubbing should then be used as the accurate basis of piece-by-piece conservation record and releading

- the examination of pre-nineteenth century leads for any names or dates milled into the heart. Medieval leads should be retained wherever possible. If lead has to be replaced consideration should be given to the melting down and recasting for reuse of lead stripped from the original panel, with the cost adjusted accordingly

- the careful choice of width of came, either to the dimensions of the original or to distinguish between major cut-lines and mending leads for legibility of design

- the considered colour-matching of any new glass to be inserted into the glazing,

taking into account both the interior and exterior effect

- the instruction of a stone mason to stand by and assist in deglazing where the glass is cemented into the glazing groove, or where the masonry frame is physically fragile, to ensure minimal damage to stonework and glass during the whole process

- liaison between the glazier and the mason, blacksmith, or carpenter, as appropriate, to make certain that adequate measurements, templates, mouldings, and glazing grooves exist to reinstate glazing accurately, and as closely as possible to its pre-removal state

- clear instructions to each specialist craftsman to clarify who is responsible for each process at each stage of the operation – and whose insurance is carrying the risk

An architect's specification should describe the means for protecting removed stained glass panels when being transported to and from the workshop, and should always ensure the adequate protection of all historically important glass which is to

Fig 76 Plastic sheeting fixed by screws and battens into the stonework. The length of the sheets has dictated the unfortunate overlap at the apex: there are no subdivisions to allow flexibility and no internal ventilation. The bird droppings do not wash off plastic through the action of wind and rain as they do with glass, but etch into the surface. This, combined with the perceptible loss of lucency through the plastic becoming opaque from exposure to sunlight, disfigures both the exterior and interior of the building (photo Jill Kerr)

remain *in situ* during works to any part of the structure. The essential rule should be observed that prevention is invariably better (and cheaper) than cure; good site management must always ensure that stones or other potential missiles are not left in the vicinity of unprotected historic glass. In choosing external protective glazing, each current method should be carefully analysed in terms of its advantages and disadvantages in relation to a particular case.

Repair of plain and decorative plasterwork

Non-hydraulic lime is the basis for most traditional plaster used internally, as it is for most traditional external renders.

Gypsum was used for plaster from the mid thirteenth century but only to a relatively limited extent. By the second half of the eighteenth century ornament was often cast in gypsum plaster, while from the beginning of the nineteenth century it came to be more generally used for wall and ceiling plasterwork, and various patented varieties were introduced, such as Keene's Cement (1838) and Parian Cement (1846). Metal lathing was introduced in the late nineteenth century but wooden lathing continued in use for ceilings until the period prior to the Second World War.

Hair is the traditional reinforcing material for the undercoats of both lime and gypsum plasters and may still be obtained for the purpose, but care must be taken that it is of sufficient length and strength. Goat hair is likely to be the most suitable. Hemp may be considered as an alternative to hair.

Wall plaster

Although internal wall plasters do not suffer from direct exposure to the elements as do external renders, they may be affected by moisture in walls caused by rising damp, defective pointing, leaking downpipes, etc and all such defects should be remedied before repairs to the plaster are carried out. Where plaster is sufficiently decayed to warrant removal, the wall should be allowed to dry out for as long as possible before the plaster is replaced.

Many of the principles and practices which apply to the repair of external renders apply also to internal wall plasters (see *Repair of external render*).

Fig 77 Efflorescing salts on damp wall plaster which has been painted with emulsion, thus preventing the natural breathing allowed by limewash

The repair of early wall plaster, especially surviving medieval work, should be approached with particular care. It should not be disturbed unless this is essential, as it may retain painted decoration under later coats of limewash. If the existence of wall paintings is suspected expert advice should be obtained so that careful investigation can be carried out.

Every attempt should be made to retain early wall plaster *in situ*, eg by filleting and grouting areas which have become detached from the wall and also, possibly, by providing mechanical fixings with non-ferrous screws. Friable surfaces may be consolidated by limewater treatment.

Ceiling plaster

Analysis of defects
When defects are evident, a careful inspection should first be carried out in order to determine the cause or causes prior to formulating proposals for repair.

A ceiling should first be looked at from the floor and a diagrammatic plan made with any obvious defects marked on it. A closer inspection should then be made of the underside from a ladder or platform to determine the seriousness of any cracks (eg their width or whether one side is lower than

Fig 78 Ceiling plaster viewed from above following the removal of floorboards, showing some deterioration of the plaster key

the other), and of any sagging, and whether the surface of the plaster is weak or crumbly.

The ceiling should then be inspected from above, either from a roof void or by the careful lifting of floorboarding. It will almost certainly be necessary to remove debris and dust with vacuum cleaners before a detailed inspection can be made of the condition of laths and of the plaster key.

The condition of main beams should be carefully inspected, particularly at the ends where they are built into walls, or under parapet gutters where they may be rotten due to damp penetration. Sagging or cracking in a ceiling may be caused by such defects or possibly by movement in roof trusses or supporting walls; in such cases all necessary structural repairs should be carried out. Repairs to beam ends, fractures along the length of beams, or weak joints should, wherever possible, be carried out *in situ* in order to avoid disturbing the plasterwork (see *Repair of structural timbers*).

Beams immediately above a ceiling should be inspected to see whether they are battened on the underside; if not there may be insufficient key for the plaster if laths are fixed directly to the underside of the beam or if the beam itself is simply hacked.

If there is evidence of damp staining on the plaster and it has a crumbly surface, an inspection should be made of roof coverings or plumbing pipes to determine whether leaks are occurring and the necessary repairs should then be carried out.

Common defects associated with the plaster itself and its lathing are the rusting of the nails fixing the laths to the ceiling joints, decay of the laths due to insect attack or damp penetration, and defective key because of incorrect spacing of the laths. Sometimes the plaster keys may have broken off, which may be caused by the persistent vibration of a ceiling.

Repairs
Following a careful inspection it will be possible to decide on the necessary extent of repair, for example whether local repairs will suffice or whether, if a ceiling is cracking or

sagging seriously over a large area, more comprehensive repairs are necessary.

It is usually possible to repair a ceiling in situ and this should always be the aim. There are, however, occasions when some dismantling may be necessary, if, for example, extensive repairs are necessary to supporting beams and joists or if access to the ceiling from above is difficult or impossible. In this case the plasterwork should be carefully cut into sections as defined by mouldings or ribs. Elements such as plaques, pendants, etc should, wherever possible, be removed in one piece.

Where sagging is occurring it will usually be necessary to support the ceiling from below. This may be achieved by providing a birdcage scaffolding to carry plywood panels, laid an inch or two below any projecting moulded robs or other decorative features, with the areas between packed up with cushions of foam rubber or felt rolls.

Mixes of plaster for repair work should wherever possible be based on an analysis of the existing work. It is important not to use a hard mix for repairs to a relatively soft existing plaster, as cracking and possibly detachment may occur due to their incompatibility.

If a limited area of plaster and laths has become detached from the joists, or if a moulded rib or other ornamental feature is loose, it is often possible to effect a local repair by screwing the plaster and lath into the joist from below, or into a short new piece of timber fixed across between the joists. Washers may be used to spread the area of support below the lath. The screw head should be set under the surface of the plaster with a wire gauze washer inserted to provide a key for plaster stopping. Non-ferrous fixings should be used.

Loose ribs may also be supported from above by copper-wire loops hung from metal rods above the ceiling or over any conveniently located timber supports.

Where local loss of key has occurred between laths or local areas of lath are defective, repairs may be achieved by cutting out the section of lath and forming a plaster

Fig 79 *In situ repairs to decorative plaster*

'bridge' running between joists, with copper screws fixed into the joists to provide support.

Where large areas of laths have failed it is essential that proper support for the ceiling is provided from below before any action is taken. The decayed laths should then be cut off against the joists, taking relatively small areas at a time, and after cleaning and preparing the back of the plaster to reduce suction, a bed of retarded plaster of Paris should be laid out and worked into the old plaster. Support is then provided by pressing troughs of copper-wire mesh into the new plaster and securing them to the joists at each side. A second coat of plaster should then immediately be applied before the initial coat has set.

Repairs using low-viscosity resin and glass fibre cloth in lieu of the above method should be approached with caution as this will effect a permanent bonding of the plaster and its timber supports, thus limiting future scope for action should further repairs be needed. This method will form an impervious surface and, for that reason, it is most usually applied in strips adjacent to the joists. This allows the central section of the area between the joists to 'breathe'. This method should only be applied by a specialist. It does, however, have the advantage of a considerable reduction of weight compared with the more traditional plaster of Paris method described above.

If ornamental features have been lost, new parts may be cast from moulds taken from adjacent original material and fixed up from below or hung from above by means of straps and rods fixed to the joists. If original material is not available from which to take a cast, photographic evidence may exist on which newly modelled ornament may be based after the preparation of detailed drawings. If moulds are formed from old moulded work by means of latex squeezes, the old work should first be thoroughly cleaned of old limewash, paint, etc, any minor defects repaired beforehand, and the new moulded elements sharpened up before fixing. Otherwise there will be loss of sharpness, 'life', and quality.

If cornices and other linear work were formed by running the basic outline *in situ*, and then applying cast or hand-moulded enrichments, it is particularly important to follow the same technique in repair or reinstatement. As much old work should be salvaged and refixed as possible; it is often feasible, for example, to detach old cast or moulded enrichments from a disintegrating cornice and refix them, making up the numbers as necessary on a newly run profile.

Acknowledgements

The helpful comments and advice during the preparation of the first edition are gratefully acknowledged: Andrew Anderson, Mrs Corinne Bennett, Peter Bird, Stephen Bond of the Royal Institute of Chartered Surveyors, John Bowles of the Redundant Churches Fund, Dr Ian Bristow, Mrs Patricia Brock, Peter Brownhill, Hugh Cantlie, Martin Caroe, Ian Curry, Christopher Dalton of the Redundant Churches Fund, Keith Darby, John Deal, Edward Diestelkamp of the National Trust, Anthony Drew-Edwards, Professor James Dunbar-Nasmith, John Earl, Richard Eckersley of the Department of the Environment Conservation Unit, Terry Empson of the Historic Houses Association, Harry Fairhurst, Alan Ford, Daryl Fowler, John Goom, Stanley Harrison of the National Trust, Anthony Hartridge, C J Howells of British Waterways, Phillip Hughes, Geoffrey Hutton, Ronald Jones, Colin Kerr, Michael King, Dr Derek Linstrum, John Maggs, Peter Marshall, Ingval Maxwell of Historic Buildings and Monuments, Scotland, Rodney Melville, Clive Mercer, Anthony New, Richard Oram of Historic Monuments and Buildings Branch, Department of the Environment for Northern Ireland, Thomas Overbury, Paul Pearn, Norman Phillips, Mrs Jane Priestman of British Rail, Robert Read, Michael Reardon, Trevor Roberts, Henry Rushton, Matthew Saunders of the Ancient Monuments Society, James Scott, James Simpson, Ian Stainburn, Robert Tolley, Andrew Townsend, Phillip Venning of the Society for the Protection of Ancient Buildings, David Walker of Historic Buildings and Monuments, Scotland, John Wheatley, Kenneth Wiltshire, and R A Wright of the British Wood Preserving and Damp-Proofing Association. The layout of the first edition was by Andrew McLaren.

Additional help from the following during the preparation of the second edition is also gratefully acknowledged: David Brock, Rebecca Child, John Fidler, John Figg of Ove Arup and Partners, Ray Harrison, David Heath, Ian Hume, Francis Kelly, John McAslan, Nicholas Molyneux, Arnold Root, Ron Phillips, Andrew Townsend, and Michael Wingate. The illustrations in Figs 37 and 40 are reproduced from vol 5 of *Practical Building Conservation* (1988) by John and Nicola Ashurst, *Wood, glass, and resin*, by kind permission of the publishers, Gower Technical Press.

Bibliography

General

Ashurst, N, 1994, *Cleaning historic buildings* (2 vols), London
Bowyer, J (ed), 1981 *Handbook of building crafts in conservation*, Leeds
Caroe, A D R, 1949 *Old churches and modern craftsmanship*, Oxford
Clifton-Taylor, A, 1987 *The pattern of English building*, London
Davey, A, 1986 *The care and conservation of Georgian houses*, London
Davey, N, 1961 *A history of building materials*, London
English Nature, 1991 *Bats in roofs; a guide for surveyors*, Peterborough
Everett, A, 1970 *Mitchell's building construction materials*, London
Feilden, B M, 1982 *Conservation of historic buildings*, London
Fidler, J, 1980 'Non-Destructive Surveying Techniques for the Analysis of Historic Buildings',
    ASCHB Transactions, 5, 1980, 3–10, London
Hollis, M, 1986 *Surveying buildings* (2nd edition), London
Insall, D W, 1973 *The care of old buildings today*, London
International Council on Monuments and Sites, UK Committee, 1990 *Guide to recording*, London
Michell, Eleanor, 1988 *Emergency repairs for historic buildings*, London
Pierce, R, Coey, A, and Oram, R, 1981 *Taken for granted*, London
Powys, A R, 1981 *Repair of ancient buildings*, London
Richardson, B A, 1991 *Defects and deterioration in buildings*, London
Rodwell, W, 1989 *Church archaeology*, London
Salzman, L F, 1990 *Building in England*, Oxford
Smith, J F, 1978 *A critical bibliography of building conservation*, London
Smith, L, 1985 *Investigating old buildings*, London

Structures

Building Research Establishment, 1991 Digest 361: *Why do buildings crack?*, Watford
Macgregor, J E M, 1971 *Outward leaning walls*, SPAB Technical Pamphlet, 1, London

Roof covering

Ashurst, J and N, 1988 *Practical building conservation: Metals*, English Heritage Technical Handbook
    4, Aldershot
British Standards Institution, 1970, 1988, *CP 143 Part 12: Sheet roof and wall coverings: copper (metric
    units)*, London
——, 1971 *BS 680 Part 2: Roofing slates (metric units)*, London
——, 1980 *BS 2870: Specification for rolled copper and copper alloys; sheet, strip, and foil*, London
——, 1982 *BS 1178: Specification for milled lead sheet for building purposes*, London
——, 1985 *BS 6561: Specification for zinc alloy sheet and strip for building*, London
——, 1990 *BS 5534 Part 1: Code of practice for slating and tiling (design)*, London
——, 1964 CP 143 *Part 5: Zinc*, London
Brocket, P, and Wright, A, 1986 *The care and repair of thatched roofs*, SPAB Technical Pamphlet **10**,
    London
Copper Development Association, 1985 *Copper in roofing design and installation*, Potters Bar
Darby, K, 1988 *Church roofing*, London
Lead Sheet Association, 1990/93, *Lead sheet manual, vols 1, 2, and 3*, Tunbridge Wells
West, R C, 1987 *Thatch, a manual for owners, surveyors, architects, and builders*, Newton Abbot
Zinc Development Association, 1991, *Zinc in building design*, London

Damp

Building Research Establishment, 1981 *Digest 245: Rising damp in walls: diagnosis and treatment*, Watford

Thomas, A R, 1986 *Treatment of damp in old buildings*, SPAB Technical Pamphlet, **8**, London

Timber

Ashurst, J, and N, 1988 *Practical building conservation: Wood, glass, and resins*, English Heritage Technical Handbook, **5**, Aldershot

Bravery, A F, Berrry, R W, Carefy, J K, and Cooper, D E, 1987 *Recognising wood rot and insect damage in buildings*, Watford

British Standards Institution, 1975 BS 1282: *Guide to the choice, use, and application of wood preservatives*, London

British Wood Preserving Association T1: *Fungal decay in buildings: dry rot and wet rot*, London

——, T2: *Preservative treatment of timber*, London

——, T3: *Methods of applying preservatives*, London

——, T4: *The preservation of window joinery*, London

——, T5: *Preservative treatment against wood borers*, London

Brunskill, R W, 1985 *Timber building in Britain*, London

Building Research Establishment *Digest 296: Timbers, their natural durability and resistance to preservative treatment*, Watford

——, *Digest 299: Dry rot: its recognition and control*, Watford

Charles, F W B, 1978 The timber-frame tradition and its preservation, *ASCHB Transactions*, 3, 5–28, London

Charles, F W B, and M, 1984, *Conservation of timber buildings*, London

Harris, R, 1981 *Discovering timber-framed buildings*, Shire Album 242, Aylesbury

Hewett, C A, 1980 *English historic carpentry*, London

——, 1969 *The development of carpentry 1200–1700*, Newton Abbot

Hughes, P, 1988 *Patching old floor boards*, SPAB Information Sheet, **10**, London

Macgregor, J E M, 1973 *Strengthening timber floors*, SPAB Technical Pamphlet, **2**, London

Ridout, B V, 1992 *Timber decay in buildings and its treatment*, Halesowen

Stonework

Ashurst, J, 1977 *Cleaning stone and brick*, SPAB Technical Pamphlet, **4**, London

Ashurst, J and N, 1988 *Practical building conservation: Stone*, English Heritage Technical Handbook, **1**, Aldershot

Ashurst, J, and Dimes, F G, 1977, reprinted 1984 *Stone in building its use and potential today*, London

——, 1990 *The conservation of building and decorative stone*, London

Bowley, M J, 1975 *Desalination of stone: a case study*, BRE Current Paper Series, CP 46/75, Watford

British Standards Institution, 1976 (1984) BS 5390: *Code of practice for stone masonry*, London

——, 1982 *BS 6270, Part 1: Code of practice for cleaning and surface repairs of buildings: natural stone, cast stone, and clay and column silicate brick masonry*, London

Building Research Establishment, 1975 *Digest 177: Decay and conservation of stone masonry*, Watford

——, 1983 *Digest 269: The selection of natural building stone*, Watford

——, 1985 *Digest 280: Cleaning external surfaces of buildings*, Watford

——, 1992 *Digest 370: Control of lichens, moulds, and similar growths*, Watford

Caroe, A D R, and Caroe, M B, 1984 *Stonework, maintenance, and surface repair*, London

Clifton-Taylor, A, and Ireson, A S, 1983 *English stone building*, London

Hughes, P, 1986 *The need for old buildings to 'breathe'*, SPAB Information Sheet, **4**, London

Kelly, A, 1990 *Mrs Coade's stone*, Upton-upon-Severn

Leary, E, 1983 *The building limestones of the British Isles*, London

Price, C A, 1975 *The decay and preservation of natural building stone*, BRE Current Paper, CP 1/75, Watford

——, 1981 *Brethane stone preservative*, BRE Current Paper, CP 1/81, Watford

——, 1984 'The consolidation of limestone using a lime poultice and limewater, *Adhesive and consolidants*, London, 160–2

Stone Industries, 1994 *Natural stone directory*, Worthing

Brickwork

Ashurst, J, and N, 1988 *Practical building conservation: Brick, terracotta, and earth*, English Heritage Technical Handbook, **2**, Aldershot

Bidwell, T G, 1977 *The conservation of brick buildings: the repair, alteration, and restoration of old brickwork*, London

Brunskill, R 1990 *Brick building in Britain*, London

Building Research Establishment, 1991 *Digest 359: Repairing brick and block masonry*, Watford

Lloyd, N, 1983 *A history of English brickwork*, Woodbridge

Williams, G B A, 1976 *Chimneys in old buildings*, SPAB Technical Pamphlet, **3**, London

——, 1983 *Pointing stone and brick walling*, SPAB Technical Pamphlet, **5**, London

Terracotta and faience

Ashurst, J and N, 1988 *Practical building conservation: Brick, terracotta, and earth*, English Heritage Technical Handbook, **2**, Aldershot

British Standards Institution, 1982 *BS 6270, Part 1: Code of practice for cleaning and surface repair of natural stone, cast stone, and clay and calcium silicate brick masonry*, London

Fidler, J, 1981 'The conservation of architectural terracotta and faience', *ASCHB Transactions*, **6**, 3–16, London

Prudhon, T H M, 1978 'Architectural terra cotta: analysing the deterioration problems and restoration approaches, *Technology and Conservation*, **3**, 30–8, London

Render

Ashurst, J, 1983 *Mortar, plasters, and renders in conservation*, London

Ashurst, J and N, 1988 *Practical building conservation: Plasters, mortars, and renders*, English Heritage Technical Handbook, **3**, Aldershot

Building Research Establishment, 1981 *Digest 196: External rendered finishes*, Watford

Cliver, E B, 1977 'Text for the analysis of mortar samples', *API Bulletin*, **VI**, No1, 68–73, London

Schofield, J, 1986 *Basic limewash*, SPAB Information Sheet, **1**, London

Townsend, A, 1989 *Roughcast for historic buildings*, SPAB Information Sheet, **11**, London

Wingate, M, 1994 *An introduction to building limes*, SPAB Information Sheet, **9**, London

Earth walls

Ashurst, J and N, 1988 *Practical Building Conservation: Brick, terracotta, and earth*, English Heritage Technical Handbook, **2**, Aldershot

Devon Earth-Building Association, 1993 *Appropriate plasters, renders, and finishes for cob and random stone walls in Devon*, Exeter

Harrison, J R, 1984 'The mud wall in England at the close of the Vernacular era', *Transactions of the Ancient Monuments Society*, **28**, London

Hughes, R, March 1983 'Material and structural behaviour of soil constructed walls', *Momentum*, 175–88, London

McCann, J, 1983 *Clay and cob buildings*, Shire Album 105, Aylesbury

Pearson, G, 1992 *Conservation of clay and chalk buildings*, London

Reinforced concrete

Dinardo, C and Ballingall, J R, 1988 'Major concrete repairs and restoration of factory structure: Uniroyal Ltd, Dumfries, Scotland', *The Structural Engineer*, **66**, No 10, London

Ironwork

British Standards Institution, 1972 *CP 3012: Cleaning and preparation of metal surfaces*, London
——, 1977 *BS 5493: Code of practice for protective coating of iron and steel structures against corrosion*, London
Evans, V R, 1972 *The rusting of iron: cause and control*, London
Hawkes, P W, 1971 'Paints for architectural cast iron', *APT Journal*, **XI**, 17–35, London
Hoever, O, 1975 *A handbook of wrought iron from the Middle Ages to the end of the eighteenth century*, London
Lister, R, 1960 *Decorative cast ironwork in Great Britain*, London

Historical glass

Burygone, I, and Scobie, R, 1983 *Two thousand years of flat glass-making*, St Helen's
Dodsworth, R, 1982 *Glass and glass-making*, Shire Album 83, Aylesbury
Harrison, Caviness, M, date? *Stained glass before 1540 An annotated bibliography*, Boston, Massachusetts
Kerr, J, 1988 'The repair and maintenance of historic glass', in *Practical building conservation: Wood, glass, and resins* (J and N Ashurst), English Heritage Technical Handbook, **5**, Aldershot
Lee, L, Seddon, G, and Stephens, F, 1976 *Stained glass*, London
McGrath, R and Frost, A C, 1961 *Glass in architecture and decoration*, London
Newton, R G, 1982 *The deterioration and conservation of painted glass: A critical bibliography*, Corpus Vitrearum, Medii Aevi Great Britain, Occasional Paper II, Oxford
Van den Bemden, Y, and De Henau, P, 1987 *Les vitraux anciens ¸ notre technique visant a l'establissement d'un cahier des charges type pour la restauration des vitraux anciens et de valeur*, Brussels

Plasterwork

Ashurst, J, 1983 *Mortars, plasters, and renders in conservation*, London
Ashurst, J and N, 1988 *Practical building conservation: Plasters, mortars, and renders*, English Heritage Technical Handbook, **3**, Aldershot
Beard, G, 1983 *Stucco and decorative plasterwork in Europe*, London
Drury, P J, 1984 'Jose Rose Senior's workshops at Audley End: Aspects of the development of decorative plasterwork technology in Britain during the eighteenth century', *Antiquaries Journal*, **LXIV**, 62–83, London
Pegg and Stagg, 1976 *Plastering ¸ a craftsman's encyclopedia*, London
Stagg, W D, and Mastons, R, 1983 *Decorative plasterwork: its repair and restoration*, London

Paint

Bristow, I, 1981a 'The redecoration of the Dulwich Picture Gallery 1980–81', *ASCHB Transactions*, **6**, 33–6, London
——, 1981b 'Repainting eighteenth-century interiors, *ASCHB Transactions*, **6**, 25–33, London
——, 1984 'The casino at Marino, part II: An account of the technical investigation of the paintwork and redecoration of the interior, *ASCHB Transactions*, **9**, 29–44, London
——, 1986a *Redecorating your church*, London
——, 1986b 'The restoration of Sir John Soane's colour scheme in the breakfast room at Pitzhanger Manor, Ealing', *ASCHB Transactions*, **11**, 43–8
Building Research Establishment, 1990 *Digest 354: Painting exterior wood*, Watford
Schofield, J, 1986 *Basic limewash*, SPAB Information Sheet, **1**, London
Thornton, P, 1984 *Authentic decor*, London